LONDON

NICK HANNA

NEW
HOLLAND

This edition published in 1999
by New Holland Publishers (UK) Ltd
London • Cape Town • Sydney • Auckland
First published in 1997
10 9 8 7 6 5 4

24 Nutford Place, London W1H 6DQ
United Kingdom

80 McKenzie Street, Cape Town 8001
South Africa

14 Aquatic Drive, Frenchs Forest NSW2086
Australia

218 Lake Road, Northcote, Auckland
New Zealand

ISBN 1 85974 064 2

Consultant: Peter Matthews
Commissioning Editor: Tim Jollands
Manager Globetrotter Maps: John Loubser
Managing Editors: Clive During, Sean Fraser
Editors: Catherine Mallinick, Gill Gordon, Rowena Curtis
Design and DTP: Sonya Cupido, John Loubser
Cartographers: William Smuts, Eloise Moss
Compiler/Verifier: Elaine Fick
Reproduction by Hirt & Carter (Pty) Ltd, Cape Town
Printed and bound in Hong Kong by Sing Cheong
Printing Co. Ltd.

Although every effort has been made to ensure
accuracy of facts, telephone and fax numbers in this
book, the publishers will not be held responsible for
changes that occur at the time of going to press.

Cover Photographs:
Top left: *The Houses of Parliament, one of London's
best-known sights.*
Top right: *Trooping the Colour: pageantry at its best.*
Bottom left: *Harrods – renowned the world over.*
Bottom right: *Tower Bridge, with HMS Belfast,
which is now a floating museum.*
Title Page: *Westminster by night.*

CONTENTS

1
Introducing London

'When a man is tired of London he is tired of life', wrote Samuel Johnson – a sentiment which is no less true today than it was in the 18th century. It is one of the great capitals of the world, the largest city in Europe, and the central focus of politics, the arts, entertainment, the media, the judiciary and much else in Britain itself.

For the visitor, London offers an endless pageant of history and tradition combined with the excitement of the avant-garde, a dizzying variety of entertainment, innumerable sporting events, a surprising number of parks and green spaces, culinary offerings that encompass almost every cuisine under the sun, and, of course, a vast plethora of shops.

The well-known highlights – such as the Tower of London, Buckingham Palace, St Paul's Cathedral and other major monuments – attract scores of tour buses, but London also has many hidden corners which repay exploration, characterful backstreets which evoke the London of Charles Dickens, wonderful riverside or canal walks, unusual specialty museums, and tranquil Georgian squares.

Like any big city, London has its problems – traffic jams and pollution, litter, and a growing number of the dispossessed and homeless – and the weather may not be the best in the world, but it still manages to extend a warm welcome to its 20 million annual visitors. It is a place which everyone has to visit at least once in their lifetime, and in so doing you will discover one of the most dynamic, vibrant and exciting cities in the world.

TOP ATTRACTIONS

*** British Museum: the city's most popular attraction boasts 6 million annual visitors.
*** The National Gallery: one of the world's most important art collections.
*** Tower of London: living history in this medieval fortress.
*** St Paul's Cathedral: an enduring symbol in the heart of the city.
*** South Kensington museums: the city's finest.
*** Westminster Abbey: resting place of the monarchs.

Opposite: *The Royal Carriages leave Buckingham Palace prior to the State Opening of Parliament.*

THE LAND

In geological terms, most of the southeast of England is relatively young and dates back to between 135 and 70 million years ago. London itself lies mostly over sand and clay (in the north) and chalk and flint (in the south). Its defining geographical feature is the **River Thames**, which bisects the city and flows out via the Thames Estuary to the North Sea.

Above: *Running through the heart of London, the River Thames has always played a crucial role in the city's history.*

The Thames

In prehistoric times the 16km (10 mile) wide **Thames Valley** offered fertile soils, extensive woodlands and a plentiful water supply to the early settlers. The core of the city, dating back to Roman times, developed at the point nearest the mouth of the Thames, where it was both feasible to build bridges and to anchor large ships in deep water. The Thames is a **tidal** river, and extensive areas on either side of its banks are classified as flood plains. In Roman times, areas to the south of the river (such as today's Lambeth and Southwark) were swampy marshes and frequently inundated. Over the centuries the southeast of England has been gradually tilting towards the sea, and central London would still be subject to flooding from surge tides were it not for the recently-built **Thames Barrier** (*see* p. 103).

London was the first capital in the world to experience the Industrial Revolution, and the banks of the Thames are crammed with vestiges of the city's heyday as the centre of the British Empire.

Climate

London has a temperate climate, with the prevailing southwesterlies creating predominantly damp conditions. It's almost impossible to generalize about the weather in London, since it is highly changeable (perhaps this is why the weather always seems to feature so prominently in

---

THAMES TRIPS

Although the Thames's role is not as pivotal as it once was, exploring the riverside history of London is one of the great pleasures of a visit to the city. There are numerous scheduled boat services and sightseeing tours which ply the river. The main boarding points in central London are at the Tower of London, Charing Cross and Westminster. Regular services run downriver to Greenwich and the Thames Barrier all year, with extended sailings in the summer upriver from Westminster to Putney, Kew, Richmond and Hampton Court. Details can be obtained by calling the London Tourist Board's Visitorcall number for river trips and boat hire: 0839 123 432 (premium rate line).

LONDON	J	F	M	A	M	J	J	A	S	O	N	D
AVERAGE TEMP. °F	40	40	44	49	55	61	64	64	59	52	46	42
AVERAGE TEMP. °C	5	5	7	10	13	16	18	18	15	12	8	6
HOURS OF SUN DAILY	1.5	2.2	3.7	5.3	6.6	7.1	6.6	6.2	4.7	3.2	1.7	1.3
RAINFALL ins.	2.1	1.6	1.5	1.5	1.8	1.8	2.2	2.3	1.9	2.2	3	1.9
RAINFALL mm	54	40	37	37	46	45	57	59	49	57	64	48
DAYS OF RAINFALL	15	13	11	12	12	11	12	11	13	13	15	15

locals' conversations). Global climatic changes also seem to be having an impact, with unseasonal winter storms on the one hand and near-drought over the summer months on the other contributing to the unpredictability of weather forecasting. **Spring** (March, April, May) is generally a pleasant time to visit, although cold March winds and April showers can dampen the days; **summer** (June, July, August) often sees sweltering hot days (or weeks) followed by thunderstorms and overcast skies; **autumn** (September, October, November) can vary from hot, summer-like days in September to crisp, clear weather in October, with November traditionally one of the wettest months; **winter** (December, January, February) is a season you should come well prepared for, with cold conditions and rain, hail, sleet or even snow a possibility.

Plant Life

London's parks, squares and public gardens are home to a huge variety of plant life. In the Royal Parks stately oaks and other trees date back hundreds of years. **St James's Park**, east of Buckingham Palace, is one such, with a pleasing mix of hawthorn, plane and lime trees and lovely weeping willow alongside the lake. **Kensington Gardens**, by contrast, is known for its displays of colourful flower borders. **Hyde Park** has a wide variety of trees, flowers and shrubberies, with daffodils

Below: *St James's Park with Horse Guards Parade. In spring, the park is a riot of colour with white and purple crocuses.*

GOVERNING LONDON

The first step towards the creation of a governing body – the mark of a true city – was the establishment of the Metropolitan Board of Works (MBW) in 1855, which administered services such as street maintainence, sewage and lighting. In 1888 the London County Council was set up, the first directly elected ruling body for the capital. The LCC was responsible for building **County Hall**, its neoclassical headquarters (completed in 1920) opposite the Houses of Parliament.

Below: *A fallow deer buck in Richmond Park, one of London's wildlife havens.*

lining busy Park Lane during spring. **Battersea Park**, south of the river, features blooming cherry and acacia in the spring. **Richmond Park** in southwest London is renowned for its magnificent oak trees, as well as thickets of flowering rhododendrons. For plant lovers London's main Mecca is, of course, the wonderful **Royal Botanic Gardens** at Kew, where greenhouses contain everything from towering palms and epiphytes to climbers and sacred lotus plants. One of the greatest storehouses in the world for plants of all kinds, Kew has magnificent displays throughout its 900ha (2223 acres).

Wildlife

London has a surprising variety of birdlife, even though in many areas all you see are pigeons, sparrows and starlings. The parks are home to numerous species, many of them introduced. The Serpentine in Hyde Park, for instance, is a fishing ground for tufted ducks, mallards, great crested grebes, moorhens, coots, and herons. In spring, migrant birds such as willow warblers, redstarts and spotted flycatchers are often seen in the parks' woodlands. Grey squirrels (introduced from North America) are fairly ubiquitous too. The largest of the royal parks, Richmond, is home to kestrels, great spotted woodpeckers, nuthatches and other bird species, as well as deer (*see* p. 110).

Once so polluted that nothing could live in it, the Thames has been cleaned up and fish have started to recolonize it. Blackheaded, common and herring gulls may be seen dipping in it as they fish, and along the more rural areas upstream the kingfisher is in evidence as are elegant swans (protected for centuries as Crown property). Downstream, the expanses of the Thames Estuary are an important habitat for migrating birds during winter months.

HISTORY IN BRIEF

The Thames Valley was home to hunter-gatherers some 500,000 years ago, and although there were isolated settlements by the time of the **Celts** it was not until the arrival of the **Romans** that a larger, more permanent settlement was founded.

Londinium to Lundenwic

In AD43 an invasion force of four Roman legions sailed from Boulogne, landing at Richborough in Kent and overwhelming the Celtic forces along the way before building a pontoon bridge across the Thames (probably near present-day Westminster) to push further northwards. Their goal was the powerful tribal stronghold of Camulodunum (Colchester), which, once conquered, became the Roman capital.

Above: *The statue of Queen Boudicca at Westminster, a reminder of London's Roman past.*

In AD60 a major rebellion by the **Iceni** tribes, under **Queen Boudicca** (Boadicea), led to the sacking of Camulodunum and a massacre of the inhabitants of the river crossing at **Londinium**. After the defeat of the Iceni (and Boudicca's suicide) Londinium was rebuilt as the main Roman base in Britain. The port prospered and grew to become the fifth most important city in the Roman Empire until the withdrawal of the Romans in the 5th century AD.

During the 6th century the settlement – then known as **Lundenwic** – prospered once more under the Anglo-Saxons, and became a thriving port until being razed to the ground by the **Vikings** in AD851. Some 30 years later the English, led by King Alfred the Great, recaptured London, but by 1016 it had again fallen to the Danes.

The death of pious (and celibate) **Edward the Confessor** – who founded Westminster Abbey – in 1066, was soon followed by the invasion of **William the Conqueror**, who laid the foundations for the Tower of London and Windsor Castle. London's special status was re-affirmed by the election of its first **mayor** in the 12th century.

GEOFFREY CHAUCER

Born into a family of London vintners, poet **Geoffrey Chaucer** (c1342–1400) travelled widely in his many jobs – he was at various times a diplomat, customs official, member of parliament and a soldier – and the wide range of people he met contributed to his knowledge of human nature which was expounded to such good effect in *The Canterbury Tales*. This rollicking saga of pilgrims on the road to Canterbury was one of the first books to be printed and the first major work of literature in the English language.

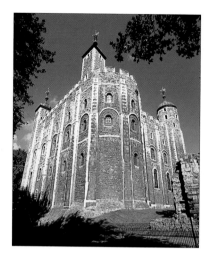

The Middle Ages

By the 14th century London's population had reached around 80,000 people but the **Black Death** (1348) wiped out over a third of the population. Economic unrest led to the **Peasant's Revolt** of 1381, a protest at the imposition of the poll tax in which Londoners opened their gates to the rebels (under Wat Tyler) and joined in the ransacking of palaces and merchants' houses.

Throughout the 15th century trade with other countries continued to expand, and the wharfs around **London Bridge** were stacked high with cargo such as wines, spices, furs, and imported cloth. Literacy was on the increase and in 1476 **William Caxton** returned from Bruges with the first printing press, which he set up at Westminster. He published over 90 books (including an edition of *The Canterbury Tales*) before his death, after which his assistant Wynkyn de Worde moved his presses to the Fleet Street area, establishing the beginnings of the printing and publishing trade in the area which was to last for several centuries.

Tudors and Stuarts

With the defeat of Richard III in the **Wars of the Roses** by Henry VII, the House of Tudor established a long-lasting peace, during which London became a centre for world commerce, with the opening up of trade routes to the Orient and the discovery of America. During the reign of **Henry VIII** the Royal Navy was established and the Church of England split from Rome – the **Reformation**, as it was known, was instigated by the king, who wanted to divorce his first wife, Catherine of Aragon. During the Dissolution of the Monasteries (1536) which followed, scores of churches and monasteries in the capital were ransacked; many were then converted to secular use by the Tudor nobility.

ELIZABETHAN THEATRE

The 'golden age' of the Elizabethan era led to the flowering of literature and drama and the rise of playwrights and authors such as William Shakespeare, Ben Jonson and Christopher Marlowe. The first theatre performances took place on temporary stages outside pubs, and although wildly popular were looked down upon by the city fathers as lewd and degenerate. This provoked James Burbage to construct London's first purpose-built theatre in Shoreditch, outside the City boundaries, in 1574. Later, he dismantled it to create the **Globe** in Southwark, where Shakespeare's plays were first performed.

Henry VIII built a new palace, **St James's**, seized **Hampton Court** from his former chancellor, Thomas Wolsey, and established numerous hunting areas which are today London's Royal Parks: Hyde Park, Regent's Park, Richmond Park and Greenwich Park.

Under **Elizabeth I** the country enjoyed considerable prosperity, and the establishment of the city's first trading centre, the **Royal Exchange** (built by Sir Thomas Gresham in 1567), helped shift the balance of commercial power in Europe from Antwerp to London. The establishment of joint-stock companies (such as the Levant Company, Hudson Bay Company and East India Company) facilitated the exploits of seafarers and traders such as Walter Raleigh, Francis Drake and John Hawkins. By 1600 London had grown to encompass a population of around 200,000 people.

The Tudor dynasty ended in 1603 with the death of Elizabeth. She was succeeded by James VI of Scotland, who united the two countries for the first time and became James I of England and Scotland. The continued persecution of Catholics led to the **Gunpowder Plot** on 5 November 1605, when Guy Fawkes and his fellow conspirators were caught in the act of trying to blow up the Houses of Parliament in protest.

Under James I's son, Charles I, the Crown found itself at odds with Parliament and the City and tensions increased when the king tried (unsuccessfully) to arrest five Members of Parliament in 1642: this sparked a **Civil War** with the Royalists pitched against the Parliamentarians under Oliver Cromwell. The Royalists lost, and Charles I was executed outside the Banqueting House in Whitehall on 30 January 1649.

For the next 11 years England became a Republic under Oliver Cromwell, until the **Restoration** of the monarchy under Charles II in 1660.

In 1665 London was hit by an outbreak of the **bubonic plague**, and the following year another major disaster occurred when the **Great Fire** of 1666 destroyed large areas of the city (*see* p. 74); it did, however, wipe out the last remnants of the plague.

THE PLAGUE

As London expanded, conditions became increasingly unsanitary: the Thames was not only the main highway and water supply but also the main dumping ground for sewage and effluents from the tanning, brewing and soap industries. There were outbreaks of **bubonic plague** (carried by fleas living on black rats) in 1603, 1625, 1636 and 1647, but a long, hot summer in 1665 led to an epidemic which killed around 100,000 inhabitants of the city.

Opposite: *The White Tower is at the centre of the great medieval castle of the Tower of London.*
Below: *Staple Inn in Holborn, one of the few timber-framed buildings to survive the Great Fire.*

Charles II wanted to reconstruct London along continental lines, with grand boulevards and circuses, but the intricacies of property ownership rendered this impractical. Many streets were, however, considerably widened as rebuilding went ahead – and bricks and mortar replaced the wooden houses of medieval London.

Georgian London

In 1714 the throne passed to George of Hanover, who became **George I** but never learned to speak English. Parliament gained in stature and the leader of the Whigs (Liberals), Sir Robert Walpole, effectively became the first Prime Minister. The king presented him with **No. 10 Downing Street**, which has traditionally been the Prime Minister's residence ever since.

London continued to grow, and numerous Georgian-style squares and terraces were built in Soho, Bloomsbury, Marylebone and Mayfair. The **West End** was developed as a fashionable shopping area, but squalor and poverty were also on the increase. The **East End** saw considerable deprivation and appallingly high death rates – the latter particularly fuelled by a glut of cheap gin, consumed at the rate of around two pints per week by adults and children alike. In 1751, Parliament was

forced to raise the price of gin to try and halt the epidemic. The imbalance between the rich and the poor led to high crime rates – daylight robbery in the West End was not unknown – and an increasing number of riots, one of the most serious of which was the **Gordon Riots** of 1780, which lasted for five days and led to over 300 deaths.

The 19th Century

In 1801, when the first official census was taken, London's population stood at around one million inhabitants, making it the most populous city in Europe. Over the next century it grew to nearly seven million as the city became increasingly industrialized and developed as the commercial and administrative hub of the British Empire. In 1811 the Prince Regent (later King George IV), laid out plans for Regent's Park and Regent Street with architect John Nash; the British Museum was begun in 1823, the National Gallery in 1824, and London University was founded in 1826.

During the reign of **Queen Victoria**, roads, railways and houses continued to be built across the capital, and docks were developed on the banks of the Thames. Pollution, squalor, prostitution and overcrowding were endemic in the slumlands of the East End; this was the underbelly of prosperous Victorian society which was so effectively chronicled by Charles Dickens.

The city's first railway line (from London Bridge to Greenwich) was opened in 1836, and the first underground line (between Paddington and Farringdon Road) was built in 1863. The achievements of the Victorian era were celebrated in the **Great Exhibition** (*see* p. 59) of 1851, an event which was so successful (attracting over six million visitors) that it led Prince Albert, the Queen's Consort, to establish an 'arts and science metropolis' – the foundation of today's museums in South Kensington.

Above: *Cumberland Terrace, in Regent's Park, is an elegant example of Nash architecture.*
Opposite: *Downing Street has been the residence of Prime Ministers since the mid 18th century.*

London at War
At the outbreak of **World War I** in August 1914 the crowds cheered the troops off to war, but the patriotic euphoria was short-lived as it became apparent that it was not going to be 'all over by Christmas'. The first bombs (dropped from a Zeppelin) fell on Stoke Newington in May 1915, but casualties in the capital were slight compared to the mortality rate and the horrors of the trenches in Belgium and northern France.

EDWARDIAN DECADENCE

The turn of the century in London was marked by the decadence of the Edwardian era, with flamboyant fashions and music halls all the rage, enlivening the city after the dour Victorian years. The Ritz, Harrods, the Café Royal and Selfridges opened for business, and the first motor cars were seen on the streets of the capital. Motor buses gradually replaced the horse-drawn variety, and electric trams were introduced.

Above: *The Cabinet War Rooms, where Churchill and his cabinet held meetings during World War II, are now open to the public.*

THE BLITZ

During the Blitz the Luftwaffe bombed the capital for 57 consecutive nights, during which Londoners sought shelter in the underground stations or purpose-built shelters in their gardens. Firemen and thousands of volunteers fought bravely to contain the fires and rescue those buried in the rubble of their houses. The worst night came on 29 December 1940, when thousands of incendiary bombs threatened to set the capital alight. By the end of the Blitz in May 1941 over a third of the City and the East End lay in ruins; over 30,000 people had died, with 50,000 injured and 130,000 houses destroyed.

In the inter-war years London's population continued to expand. The greatest growth was in the newly created suburbs, particularly to the north. The voting franchise was extended to all males over 21 years of age and females over 30, although it was not until 1928 that universal suffrage was achieved. Previously the vote had been restricted to the landed gentry, middle-class professionals, and 'settled tenants' (workers in towns).

In an attempt to emulate the success of the Great Exhibition, the British Empire Exhibition was held at Wembley in 1924–5, but its displays of the wealth and might of the Empire were overshadowed by a looming Depression. A confrontation between mine-owners and the unions led to the **General Strike** of 1926, with London in a state of near anarchy for nine days until the strike leaders caved in.

At the outbreak of **World War II** in 1939 trench shelters were dug in London's parks, over 600,000 women and children were evacuated to the countryside, and the strict enforcement of night-time black-outs led to a huge increase in road accidents. But the bombs didn't arrive for another year, with the beginning of the **Blitz** in September 1940, marked by many deaths and thousands injured.

Post-war Years

Victory in Europe (VE) Day in 1945 was followed by a General Election, where Winston Churchill was defeated by Clement Attlee's Labour Party. The Welfare State was created and the government embarked on wholesale nationalization of key industries, but in the capital the most pressing problem was a shortage of houses: pre-fabricated buildings were erected all over the city and massive high-rise housing estates were built on derelict bomb sites. In an attempt to relieve the austerity of day-to-day life, the **Festival of Britain** was staged in 1951 on the south bank of the Thames; the site eventually became the South Bank Centre.

During the 1950s the population of the capital fell, although there was also a large influx of immigrants from the former colonies and the Caribbean. The '**Swinging Sixties**' heralded a new era of liberation and 'groovy' London became the music and fashion capital of the world.

The 1970s seemed drab by comparison, with economic austerity leading to the three-day week in 1974 and the downfall of the Conservative government. Britain became part of the EEC, and the IRA started a long bombing campaign on the mainland. At the end of the 1970s **Margaret Thatcher** swept to power and began a process of privatization and cuts in public services which was to leave few areas untouched.

In 1986 the stock market was deregulated (the 'Big Bang') but the boom which followed was short-lived, and the crash of the money markets in 1987 led to a deepening recession which was exacerbated by a slump in property prices in 1988. In 1990, riots in Trafalgar Square against the **poll tax** signalled the beginning of the end for Margaret Thatcher, who was replaced as leader of the Conservative Party by John Major in October of that year. The seven years of growing dissatisfaction with Conservative rule that followed led to Tony Blair and his New Labour Party sweeping into power in May 1997.

A number of grandiose building schemes are currently taking shape, many of them funded by the National Lottery. Among them are the controversial Millennium Dome in Greenwich and the conversion of Bankside Power Station into the Tate Gallery of Modern Art.

SOCIAL UNREST

During the Thatcher years social polarities in the capital increased, with stark contrasts between the huge increase in long-term unemployment and the conspicuous consumption enjoyed by the professional classes ('yuppies'). Riots erupted in Brixton in 1981 and Tottenham in 1985, and homelessness in the capital reached levels not witnessed since Victorian times. An area around the South Bank became known as 'Cardboard City' due to the number of vagrants living in cardboard shelters on the pavements.

Below: *The Royal Festival Hall, on the South Bank, is at the heart of London's most popular arts complex.*

GOVERNMENT AND ECONOMY

The UK is a constitutional monarchy, with the seat of Government based in London. Britain has no written constitution (a subject much debated in recent years) and theoretically the Queen has the power to veto legislation, although her approval for new laws nowadays is more of a formality than anything else. The Government of the day is led by the Prime Minister and his Cabinet of key ministers, who place legislation before Parliament for ratification. Sitting in the Palace of Westminster, Parliament consists of the 659 elected Members of the House of Commons and the unelected House of Lords; the latter (consisting of around 1200 members) is frequently condemned as an anachronism and no longer has the power to veto laws as it once did.

Local government

In 1965 the London County Council (*see* p. 8) was replaced by the **Greater London Council** (GLC), which controlled the entire 1580km^2 (610,000 sq miles) of Greater London and was responsible for a wide range of services and strategic planning. The GLC, however, found itself increasingly at odds with central Government, a situation which reached its peak under the socialist GLC leader, 'Red Ken' Livingstone, in the 1980s. The GLC's introduction of subsidized public transport policies was anathema to the Thatcher government, who responded by abolishing the GLC in 1986. So far, London remains the only capital in Europe with no overall governing body. In May 1998 a referendum decided that Greater London should have an elected mayor and its own assembly, responsible for transport, fire, police and other services.

Economy

London continues to dominate in the political and financial arenas and leads the UK in many other areas including the arts, culture, fashion, publishing, retailing, the media and much else besides. Tourism is an important component of the service economy, with over 20 million annual visitors.

Although London is home to just 12% of the UK's population, it accounts for 15% of GDP (Gross Domestic Product); the GDP per capita is 26% higher than the national average.

Service industries (employing some 700,000 people) make up the largest share of the metropolitan economy, with the concentration of financial, professional and business services reflecting the city's international role. But London is still a major manufacturing centre, with output which exceeds, for example, that of Denmark, Italy or Greece. Manufacturing accounts for 13% of London's GDP, and 333,000 jobs: pharmaceutical and medical research are particularly strong, with 46 of the world's top 50 pharmaceutical companies based in London or the Southeast.

London is the longest established of the world's three primary financial centres, and is the world's largest centre for foreign exchange trading, international bank lending, derivatives, reinsurance and Eurobonds. Eight of Europe's top 10 law firms are located in the city, reflecting the importance of London as a centre for international arbitration. As a centre for media and creative industries, it boasts a quarter of Europe's top 100 media companies.

London's standing as a global centre for international business is likely to be further enhanced as Britain integrates more fully into Europe.

Above: *The skyline of the City of London, a mosaic of modern architecture, is very impressive at night.*
Below: *The sumptuous interior of the stately House of Lords.*
Opposite: *The gilded statue of Justice sits atop the Old Bailey, or Central Criminal Court.*

Above: *The annual Notting Hill Carnival is the largest street festival in Europe.*

LONDON'S POPULATION

12th century Beginnings of the capital: 18,000.
14th century Beginnings of overseas trade: 50,000.
1348 Black Death wipes out half the population.
16th century Boom times under the Tudors: 200,000.
1664–1665 Great Plague kills 70,000–100,000.
1700 London is Europe's most populous city: 575,000.
1801 First official census: One million.
1900 Victorian expansion swells the city: 6–7 million.
1939 Peak inter-war population: 8.7 million.
1940–41 30,000 killed in Blitz.
1950s Immigration from former colonies: 20,000 annual arrivals.
1960s–70s Decline of manufacturing and flight to the suburbs: 500,000 leave the capital.
1996 Population: c.7 million.

THE PEOPLE

For centuries London has been a cosmopolitan city, attracting people from other nations to live and work here. Refugees, traders, artists and others over the generations have flocked to what John Milton dubbed the 'mansion-house of liberty', and today you will find not only the Irish (during the 19th century there were already over 100,000 Irish in London), Italians, Bangladeshis, Germans and West Indians but also Kurds, Somalis, Moroccans, Portuguese and people from every corner of the globe. One in five of London's 7 million residents belongs to a minority ethnic group and no less than 33 countries have resident communities of over 10,000 people who were born outside the UK and now live in the capital.

It is estimated that 200 languages are spoken in the city, and it is claimed that over 30% of Londoners are descended from first-, second- and third-generation immigrants. Writer H V Morton concluded in the 1940s that 'one of the charms of London is that there are no Londoners', while Evelyn Waugh bewailed the fact that 'The English are already hard to find in London. No-one lives there who is not paid to do so . . . I believe that London society has ceased to exist.'

Ethnic London

London is by no means a homogenous entity and Londoners tend to associate more with the neighbour-hoods in which they live than with the city as a whole. There are no 'ghettos' as such, although immigrant groups have tended to settle in certain localities for par-ticular reasons: Punjabi Sikhs, for instance, populated Southall in the vicinity of Heathrow Airport because it was near their point of arrival, and the airport offered work. Cypriots gravitated to Camden and Finsbury, where they could use their skills in the clothing trade, while Bengali Muslims moved to the area around Brick Lane in Tower Hamlets for similar reasons. The Chinese, too, moved into the East End – but, curiously, it was the introduction of public launderettes which largely put paid to their traditional laundry businesses and precipitated a switch to running Chinese restaurants in Soho. The Afro-Caribbean community has traditionally been based in Brixton, to the south of the river, and Notting Hill, in the north.

London Neighbourhoods

While the 1960s witnessed some breaking down of the rigid class barriers of London society, Londoners still tend to be seen as haughty, snobbish and unfriendly by those who live in the provinces, and the smart districts – Mayfair, Knightsbridge, and Kensington – are still largely the preserve of the wealthy elite, while the East End is a steadfastly working class area. Meanwhile, from the 1970s onwards the professional classes recolonized great swathes of North London – from Hampstead to Hackney – as well as areas south of the Thames (such as Camberwell and Greenwich) and property prices soared as gentrification led to a proliferation of wine bars, delicatessens and the like alongside the renovation of 19th-century terraces. During the 1980s the upwardly-mobile 'yuppies' extended this process to Docklands, converting old warehouses into stylish 'loft apartments' and parking their Porsches in the shadow of long-defunct dockyard cranes.

Londoners tend to associate more with their locality or neighbourhood than might be imagined, venturing fort for shopping and entertainment to the West End or to the City and elsewhere to work. The City itself is a curious anomaly: formerly the heart of London, it has a daytime working population of 400,000 but a night-time population of just 4000 – an area, as it were, without resident citizens.

COCKNEYS

A 'Cockney' in the broadest sense is anyone born and bred in London, although it usually applies only to working class East End residents – traditionally, only those born within the sound of the bells of St Mary-le-Bow in Cheapside can claim to be true Cockneys. Cockney rhyming slang thrives in street markets and pubs: 'tit for tat' is a hat, 'apples and pears' are the stairs, and so on. Cockney 'Pearly Kings and Queens' put on their traditional, button-studded costumes for the Costermongers Pearly Harvest Festival Service held at the church of St Martin-in-the-Fields (Trafalgar Square) on the first Sunday in October every year. A 'costermonger' is someone who sells fruit and other produce from a market barrow, and this is essentially a harvest festival.

Below: *The 'Pearly Kings and Queens' in their traditional button-studded finery.*

SPORTING VENUES

Tickets for major international
events can be extremely hard
to come by, and you need
to book well in advance
(sometimes several months).
• Crystal Palace National
Sports Centre
(tel: 0181 778-0131);
• Lord's Cricket Ground
(tel: 0171 289-1611);
• The Oval
(tel: 0171 582-6660);
• Wembley Stadium
(tel: 0181 900-1234);
• Ascot Racecourse
(tel: 01344 622-211);
• Epsom Downs
(tel: 01372 470-047);
• Kempton Park
(tel: 01372 470-047);
• Sandown Park
(tel: 01372 470-047);
• Windsor
(tel: 01753 865-234);
• Twickenham Stadium
(tel: 0181 892-2000);
• Wimbledon All England
Lawn Tennis Club
(tel: 0181 946-2244).

It may be romanticising the cohesion of local communities too much to claim that London is a collection of villages, but architecturally and otherwise the vestiges are still there in places such as Dulwich, Highgate, and Hampstead. While it may be the largest city in Europe, London is by no means a uniform entity as regards the people and the districts which comprise this great metropolis.

Sport and Recreation

Whether you want to spectate or to become involved, there are numerous opportunities to participate in sporting activities in and around London. Many top international fixtures take place in the hallowed grounds of sporting venues such as **Lord's** (cricket), **Wimbledon** (tennis), **Crystal Palace** (athletics), **Wembley Stadium** (football/soccer), and **Twickenham** (Rugby Union). In addition, world-famous horse races take place at locations such as **Ascot**, **Epsom**, and **Sandown Park**.

For those who want to do more than just watch, London offers opportunities for the sporty to take part in everything from aerobics to windsurfing. Council-run facilities provide inexpensive access to sports such as tennis, swimming, weight-training, aerobics and so on.

There are also numerous private gymnasia and health clubs, including those in major hotels. London's parks, of course, offer opportunities for jogging, walking, tennis or boating in the lush green outdoors.

Athletics: Major international events, as well as local contests, take place at the **Crystal Palace National Sports Centre**, with the two biggest competitions in early summer (June/July) and late summer (August).

Cricket: The cricket season runs from April to September. England's national game may seem as if it is dominated by arcane rules and peculiar terminology ('silly mid-offs', 'yorkers', 'googlies', and so on) but even the uninitiated will derive pleasure from watching the game played at its best on a sunny weekend afternoon. The biggest drawcards of the season are the international **test matches** between England and touring teams, one of which is always played at **Lord's Cricket Ground** (the home of the Middlesex County Cricket Club) in St John's Wood, and another at **The Oval** in Kennington.

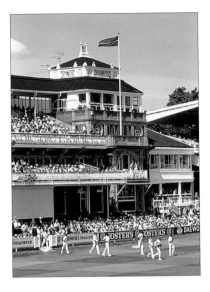

Football: Football (soccer) probably arouses more passion in the English than any other game, and although it is usually the big northern clubs which dominate the league tables, London prides itself on the strength of its teams such as Arsenal ('the Gunners'), Tottenham Hotspur (Spurs) and Chelsea. The season is from mid-August to early May, culminating in the FA Cup Final at Wembley Stadium.

Horse Racing: A day at the races provides an entertaining insight into the personalities of the British people from all walks of life, with a flutter on the filly of your choice adding excitement to the occasion. Major race courses within easy reach of London include **Ascot** (with the highlight being the glamorous Royal Ascot meeting in June), **Epsom** (one of the world's fastest courses, home to Derby Day in June), **Kempton Park** (where meetings are far less snobby than elsewhere), **Sandown Park** (popular for day trips from the capital), and **Windsor** (which has quite a delightful setting alongside the Thames).

Rugby: There are two kinds of rugby (or rugger) played in Britain, **Rugby Union** (15-a-side) and **Rugby League** (13-a-side). In London there is one Rugby League team (the London Broncos), with other major teams (such as the Wasps, Harlequins and London Irish) playing Rugby Union. The season runs from September to April/May, culminating in the **Pilkington Cup** (the equivalent of the FA Cup Final), held at the end of April at the modern and impressive **Twickenham Stadium** in West London.

Above: *Lord's Cricket Ground, in St John's Wood, is one of London's most famous sporting venues.*
Opposite: *Around 35,000 people take part in the annual London Marathon.*

LONDON MARATHON

Held in March/April, the London Marathon follows a 40km (25 mile) course from Greenwich to Westminster and annually attracts around 35,000 participants. To participate, you must book before the end of September in the previous year. Details from the marathon hotline, tel: (0891) 334 450 (premium rate line).

Right: *Wimbledon is the setting for the famous lawn tennis championships.*

Tennis: The climax of the international tennis season is the Grand Slam championship tournament, played on the famous grass courts at **Wimbledon** during the last week of June and the first week of July. Almost as famous for the cost of off-court strawberries as for the on-court antics of the international stars, tickets for the 'Wimbledon fortnight' are notoriously hard to obtain.

The Arts

Architecture: The only vestiges of **Roman** Londinium are parts of the old Roman wall (visible at Tower Hill) and the ruins of the Temple of Mithras. **Norman** buildings are represented by the Tower of London and the church of St Bartholomew the Great in Smithfield, and the undercroft of Westminster Abbey. Most of the Abbey was rebuilt from the 13th century onwards in the **Medieval Gothic** style, other examples of which include Southwark Cathedral. The **Tudor** style tended to favour red brick over stone, with the most outstanding examples being Hampton Court Palace and St James's Palace.

The **English Renaissance** is best exemplified by the work of Inigo Jones, responsible for the Queen's House at Greenwich, the Banqueting House at Westminster, and the piazza in Covent Garden. The other great architect of the era was Sir Christopher Wren: following the Great Fire in 1666, Wren rebuilt St Paul's Cathedral and no less than 51 other churches in the City, as well as the

---

HAPHAZARD PLANNING

London may have some of the finest architecture in the world but the city itself has developed over the centuries in a random fashion, with none of the great set pieces or rational planning of other major cities. The two focal points of its growth since medieval times are the City of London and Westminster, with development since the 18th century sprawling outwards to encompass a series of 'villages' which now form part of the huge conglomeration which is Greater London. One of the few set pieces of planning was John Nash's venture to create a fine boulevard (Regent Street) linking Piccadilly Circus (known as Regent Circus until 1880) with the former Marylebone Park, known as Regent's Park today.

Old Royal Observatory at Greenwich, the Royal Hospital in Chelsea, and numerous other famous landmarks. During the 18th century the neoclassical style was fashionable, when designer **Robert Adam** remodelled mansions such as Kenwood House, Osterley Park and Syon House. It was during this period that John Nash laid out Regent Street, linking St James's Palace with Regent's Park. The legacy of the **Georgian** period can be seen in the numerous elegant terraced houses which still exist in areas such as Bloomsbury, Islington, Greenwich, Dulwich and Hampstead.

During the **Victorian** era London was transformed by the building of new roads, railways, bridges, canals and docks. Prestigious buildings of this period (some harking back to the neoclassical or even Gothic traditions) include the British Museum, the Houses of Parliament, the National Gallery, Tower Bridge, the Natural History Museum and St Pancras Station. **Edwardian** London gave us the Old Bailey and department stores such as Selfridges and Harrods. The city has few buildings from the **Modernist** era, and although there were once scores of Art Deco cinemas, most have been demolished.

The **Post-War** period saw the building of the Royal Festival Hall, the unusual Commonwealth Institute, and dozens of concrete tower blocks (many of which are now being pulled down). Concrete also predominated in the construction of the South Bank Complex and the Barbican Centre complex.

In recent years most of the **Post-Modernist** architecture has been concentrated in the City and Docklands, with notable architecture including the controversial Lloyds of London, Cesar Pelli's Canary Wharf tower and the Broadgate development next to Liverpool Street Station. Other remarkable buildings include the London Ark in Hammersmith, the stunning Waterloo International Terminal, the controversial new British Library, and the Channel 4 Television building.

THE WHITE CARD

If you're planning on visiting several of the capital's top art galleries and museums you can save money on entrance fees by purchasing an all-inclusive pass, called the White Card. Participating venues include the Barbican Art Gallery, Courtauld Galleries, Design Museum, Hayward Gallery, Museum of the Moving Image, most South Kensington Museums, and several others. The card is valid for periods of 3 or 7 days and for individuals costs £16 (3 days) or £26 (7 days); for families (2 adults and up to four children) £32 (3 days) or £50 (7 days). Available from Tourist Information Centres or your hotel concierge.

Below: *The Art Deco Broadcasting House, home of the BBC's national radio services, was built in 1931.*

THEATRE TOURS

If you want to find out more about what goes on in some of London's famous theatres, you can take backstage tours (duration from 30 to 75 minutes) of several major theatres including the Royal National Theatre, (South Bank Centre, tel: (0171) tours 452-3400, box office 452-3000); the Theatre Royal, Drury Lane (Catherine St, WC2; tel: (0171) 494-5091); Theatre Royal, Haymarket (tel: (0171) 930-8800). All tours should be booked in advance.

Below: *The Royal Academy, on Piccadilly, holds several exhibitions each year.*

Art: For the art lover, London offers not only some of the world's greatest collections of western art but also a thriving contemporary scene with a huge range of new, creative talent on display. The historic collections of the National Gallery, Tate Gallery, Courtauld Institute, the British Museum and the Victoria and Albert Museum will provide sufficient riches to sustain even the most ardent enthusiast.

In modern art, London has a number of dynamic young artists (names to watch out for include Damien Hirst, Helen Chadwick, Mat Collishaw, Fiona Rae and Anya Gallacio, amongst others) whose work can often be seen – for free – in the **commercial galleries** of Dering and Cork streets, both in the West End. The **Summer Exhibition** at the Royal Academy mostly features amateur artists, but the often controversial **Turner Prize** exhibits, which are displayed at the Tate Gallery in the month preceding the judging (November), are worth seeing. Another avenue to explore is the summer **degree shows** held at the various London art colleges in late May/June, in particular those at Goldsmiths, the Royal College, the Royal Academy, the Slade, and St Martin's School of Art.

Theatre: With a stage history that dates back to the father of theatre, William Shakespeare, it is little wonder that London is often considered the theatre capital of the world. While the West End may appear to be dominated by blockbusting musicals, numerous other stages provide the platform for inventive, talented work and original productions. London is home to two great acting companies, the **Royal Shakespeare Company** and the **Royal National Theatre**, but stars of the stage (and screen) can also be seen in numerous productions away from the West End or mainstream theatres. In addition, there is a thriving **fringe theatre** scene, with avant-garde plays staged in locations as diverse as pubs and converted warehouses.

In any one week there
may be around 200 shows
on the go, so you will be
spoilt for choice.
**Classical Music, Opera
and Dance:** London has
a number of venues for
classical music, ranging
from the ornate splendour
of the **Royal Albert Hall**
to the three, purpose-built
halls of the **South Bank
Centre**, the acoustically

perfect **Wigmore Hall**, and the **Barbican Centre** complex, and on any one day there are likely to be several
performances to choose from. The capital is home to the
Royal Philharmonic Orchestra, the **London Symphony
Orchestra**, the **London Philharmonic Orchestra**, the
Philharmonia, and the **BBC Symphony Orchestra**, to
name but the most prominent. Concerts are, in many
cases, poorly attended (to the shame of Londoners), so
there is rarely a problem getting tickets. You can take
advantage of free **lunchtime concerts** from Monday
to Friday in many churches (such as St Martin-in-the-
Fields, St James's Church in Piccadilly, and several
others in the City area). Outdoor concerts are also held
at **Kenwood House** in the summer (*see* p. 89); a wide
range of works is also performed during the **Henry
Wood Promenade Concerts**, 'The Proms', (*see* p. 67)
during the summer months.

Opera was first staged at the **Royal Opera House**
in 1817, and performances still pack the house despite
the exorbitant ticket prices. The opera house will close
from July 1997 until the end of 1999 for redevelopment.
During this period performances will be held at alternative venues. More reasonably priced performances can
be seen at the **London Coliseum**, home to the **English
National Opera**. New and innovative works are often
performed during the summertime **Almeida Opera
Festival** at the **Almeida Theatre** in Islington (*see* p. 91).

Above: *Popular theatre
productions can run for
decades. The Mousetrap
is the longest running play
in the world.*

BRIGHT LIGHTS, BIG CITY

The quality and variety of
London's arts, culture and
entertainment scene is probably unrivalled anywhere in
the world. To navigate your
way around this cultural
maze, the most comprehen-
sive listings of what's on are
found in the weekly *Time Out*,
while the *Evening Standard*
on Fridays and on Saturdays
(in its *Review* section) will
also provide a few pointers.
Information is also available
from the Tourist Board
Visitorcall service:
• Popular West End Shows
(tel: 0839 123-416);
• Productions beyond the
West End
(tel: 0839 123-434);
• Rock and Pop Concerts
(tel: 0839 123-422);
• Current Exhibitions
(tel: 0839 123-403).

Dance in all its varied forms is well represented in the capital, with every style from the classic showpieces of the **Royal Ballet** to contemporary works and even Brazilian or Indian dance on display. Major venues include the **ICA**, the **London Coliseum**, the **Royal Opera House**, **Riverside Studios** (Hammersmith), and the **South Bank Centre**. In addition, regional and international touring companies often perform in London. One of the best showcases for new talent is the annual **Dance Umbrella** festival, held in October/November.

Above: *Tea at the Ritz is a British institution.*

AFTERNOON TEA

Afternoon tea is another great British institution which shouldn't be missed. Mostly the speciality of the grand hotels, the set tea usually involves 'finger' sandwiches (smoked salmon, cucumber and the like) followed by assorted cakes, scones with cream, or pastries, served with a selection of teas. Most of the big hotels have dress codes (no jeans or trainers) and in some (such as the Ritz) such is the popularity of afternoon tea that advance bookings are required.

Food and Drink

British food may once have been something of an international joke, epitomized by things like comforting, stodgy pies and puddings ('nursery food'), greasy fish and chips, and mammoth fry-ups for breakfast. But that is an image which is well past its sell-by date, particularly in London, where the range of cuisines available is huge and the variety of eateries (from pubs to trendy cafés, brasseries, wine bars, bistros and the like) has expanded enormously in recent years. Coupled with this, there has been a revolution in top-end gourmet restaurants where home-grown talent is now proving itself to be a match for the best anywhere else in the world. Whatever your budget or taste buds dictate, you can be sure that London will provide plenty of culinary adventures.

The most characteristic British drinking venue is, of course, the 'public house' or **pub**, a social institution which stretches back to the days of wayside coaching inns. London has a vast diversity of pubs, many of them dating from the Victorian era, and there are very few places where you won't find one within handy reach. Be warned though – they can be ghastly, with plastic decor, rude staff, terrible food and gassy beer (this is particularly true in the West End, where good pubs need some ferreting out). On the other hand, the best of them will feature a good range of 'real ales' (*see* p. 29), a welcoming atmosphere, tasty snacks and an entertaining ambience. Many are still the centre of the surrounding communities, with 'locals' propping up the bar and socializing. Many more have also been refurbished and feature fringe theatre or cabaret performances, live music, and even their own on-site micro-breweries. Good food, too, has become much more important in recent years, and lunchtime is the most popular time to eat in a pub (if possible try and avoid the 13:00–14:00 crush when they're packed out with office workers).

Wine is generally best avoided in pubs, and in this case you're better off heading for a **brasserie** or **wine bar**, of which there are scores throughout the capital.
Modern British Cuisine: A new wave of restaurateurs and chefs have added spice and flair to British cuisine, proving that the capital is no longer the culinary backwater it was once thought to be – in fact, London now boasts more restaurants bearing the coveted Michelin star than any other European city apart from Paris, and on the wider scale Britain has more three-star restaurants than either Germany or Italy.

'New wave' British cuisine has chefs such as Jonathan Rickets (at Alastair Little in Soho), Matthew Harris (Bibendum, SW3), Nico Ladenis (Chez Nico at Ninety Park Lane, W1) and Gordon Ramsay (Aubergine, SW10), leading the way. There is no overall style to this new wave, apart from a consistent sense of inventiveness and an eclectic use of

> **TRADITIONAL BREAKFASTS**
>
> Traditional British breakfasts are legendary, and are usually served up to around 11:00 in hotels and cafés. The obligatory fry-up of eggs, bacon, sausage and fried bread is often supplemented at the more classy establishments by extras such as bubble and squeak, black pudding, kedgeree or kidneys. After one of these hearty breakfasts you'll be well set up for a day's sightseeing.

Below: *The City Barge Pub at Strand-on-the-Green, Chiswick: one of London's many pubs where you may enjoy a drink outside.*

FISH AND CHIPS

Once considered to be the
only worthwhile British
culinary export to the world,
fish and chips can be found
almost everywhere – but
standards vary widely. The
best fish and chips are found
in popular places such as the
Sea Shell, Rock and Sole Plaice
and the Upper Street Fish
Shop (see p. 117 for details).
There are also many excellent
seafood restaurants where
you can enjoy Dover sole,
plaice, sea bass, or even
Cockney staples such as
cockles, or eel pie and mash.

Below: *Simpson's in the
Strand is a good place to
sample traditional roast beef
and Yorkshire pudding.*

ingredients and methods which draws on everything
from West Coast/Californian to Mediterranean and Far
Eastern influences.

Entertaining Themes: Another recent phenomenon
on the London restaurant scene has been the rise of
mega entertainment and eating venues, pioneered by
style guru **Sir Terence Conran** with the opening of the
massive 350-seat Quaglino's restaurant in 1994; in 1995
he followed this with the even bigger (700-seat) Mezzo,
which is on two floors with glass-fronted kitchens,
has an in-store bakery, patisserie, café and Asiatic
food shop, as well as a vast restaurant – thought to be
the largest in Europe. Meanwhile, Marco Pierre White
has continued to expand his empire, which now
includes the Mirabelle, the Criterion Brasserie and Quo
Vadis, which is decorated with artworks by Damien
Hirst. Planet Hollywood (backed by Hollywood
heavies Sylvester Stallone, Bruce Willis and Arnold
Schwarzenegger) in Piccadilly and the Sports Café in
the Haymarket are all part of the same trend, with the

Fashion Café (also in Piccadilly and
backed by a posse of supermodels)
set to become another trendy hangout for the movers and shakers.

Traditional British Food: Alongside
the growth of 'modern British' cuisine
(see p. 27), there has also been a revival
of traditional cooking in the capital's
restaurants, with good, hearty food
thankfully banishing the excesses of
nouvelle cuisine to the culinary dust-
bin. Some restaurants, of course, never
followed fashion anyway, and places
such as the 150-year-old Simpson's in
the Strand, and the Quality Chop
House (EC1), have been serving staples such as steak and kidney pudding
and fish cakes since time immemorial.
Bangers and mash, meat casseroles
and pies, shepherd's pie, toad-in-the-

Left: *Hand-pumped beer is the hallmark of a traditional pub.*

hole and roast beef with Yorkshire pudding are just some of the main courses you might come across. Desserts include treats such as jam roly-poly, sponges, trifles, toffee pudding, spotted dick and bread-and-butter pudding.

Ethnic Restaurants: London has always been known for its ethnic cuisine, in particular Indian, Bangladeshi and Chinese food. Many of the numerous curry houses tend to churn out identical dishes (with sauces bought in bulk) which have limited appeal, but to balance this there are many excellent establishments where freshly prepared ingredients are used to good effect in regional dishes from India, Nepal, Sri Lanka, Pakistan and Bangladesh. A similar caveat applies to Chinese restaurants, where monosodium glutamate (MSG) is heaped on regardless: however, London also has some of the best Cantonese chefs in Europe (partly due to an exodus from Hong Kong before it reverted to Chinese rule in 1997), with *dim sum* (lunchtime snacks) one of the most characteristic features of the cuisine.

But the range of ethnic restaurants does not stop there, and you'll also come across African, Caribbean, Japanese, Korean, Thai, Malaysian, Indonesian, Turkish, Jewish and even Vietnamese eateries. Continental fare is well represented with French, Italian, Spanish, Greek, Portuguese and Swiss restaurants.

REAL ALES

The classic British pub drink is a pint of **bitter**, a dark, uncarbonated brew that comes in many guises. The best bitters are those pumped by hand from the cellar, and served at room temperature. In previous decades the big breweries swallowed up many traditional small brewers and imposed a uniformly bland, gassy product on many pubs: thanks to the efforts of CAMRA (the Campaign for Real Ale) this trend was halted (if not reversed), and to taste the real thing you should avoid pubs where the beer is served by electric pump. Chilled, draught **lager** and bottled lagers are also widely available in pubs, as is Guinness, a dark, creamy Irish **stout.** The main London breweries are Youngs and Fullers.

2
Whitehall and Westminster

Westminster, at the heart of the capital, has been the main seat of political and regal power for nearly a thousand years and consequently boasts some of London's most famous landmarks, such as the **Houses of Parliament**, **Big Ben** and **Westminster Abbey**. **Buckingham Palace** is nearby, as is **Trafalgar Square** with **Nelson's Column** and the **National Gallery**.

Westminster's role in the nation's history dates back to Edward the Confessor, who abandoned his predecessors' palace in the commercial heart of the city (2km/1¼ miles to the east) to build a grand church, 'West Minster', on a swampy site at the mouth of the River Tyburn, and a new palace alongside it so that he could supervise the project. The pious king died 10 days after his abbey was completed, but Westminster Palace remained as the monarch's main residence until it was damaged by fire, forcing Henry VIII to build a new one in Whitehall. The **Palace of Westminster** later became the Houses of Parliament, but Whitehall Palace burnt down in 1698, and the thoroughfare we now know as **Whitehall** – linking the Houses of Parliament with Trafalgar Square – became the preserve of government civil servants. The Prime Minister's residence is located at **Number 10 Downing Street** on its west side.

All the area's main sights are within easy walking distance of each other, and there are connections to other parts of London along the river from Westminster Pier. Westminster is rather quiet – and **Covent Garden** is the place to head for food and entertainment.

DON'T MISS

*** Westminster Abbey: with its hundreds of memorials embodying centuries of English history.
*** Buckingham Palace: Changing of the Guard. Visit the **State Rooms** in August–September.
*** Tate Gallery: contemporary art and English landscapes.
** Trafalgar Square: feed the pigeons and visit the **National Gallery**.
** Big Ben and the **Houses of Parliament:** particularly for the view from the Thames.

Opposite: *The Houses of Parliament, 'birthplace of democracy'.*

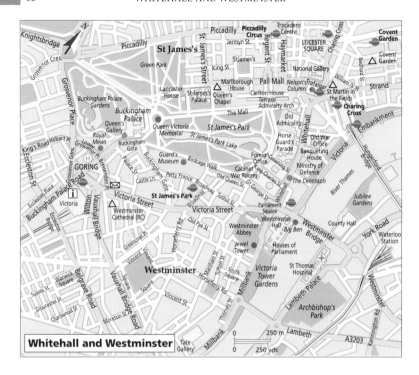

Whitehall and Westminster

ALONG WHITEHALL

This broad, 1km-long avenue links Trafalgar Square with
Parliament Square, and is lined with buildings housing
key government offices and ministries. It was named
after the former Whitehall Palace, where Henry VIII
lived for his last 14 years. The palace was destroyed by
fire in 1698, and only the **Banqueting House** (open
10:00–17:00, Monday–Saturday), which was built by
Inigo Jones for James I, remains. The wonderful ceiling
in the main dining hall was painted by Rubens. He was
commissioned by Charles I, who was put to death outside this hall in 1649. Stepping through the window on
to the scaffolding outside, he wore several shirts in case
he should shiver from the cold and the crowd mistake
this for fear. After the execution, his head was sewn back
on before the corpse was taken for burial at Windsor.

Horse Guards *

Opposite the Banqueting House is the **Horse Guards**, once the old palace guard house, where the impassive troopers of the Queen's Household Cavalry stand outside their sentry boxes or on horseback. During the celebrated Changing of the Guard (*see* p. 32), mounted troopers in full livery ride up from Hyde Park Barracks via Hyde Park Corner, to the **Horse Guards Parade** on the other side of the building, where the ceremony takes place.

10 Downing Street **

Past the Old Treasury on the same side of Whitehall as the **Horse Guards** is the home of the British Prime Minister. This modest-looking house was presented to Britain's first Prime Minister, Sir Robert Walpole, in 1732, and is connected to the home of the Chancellor of the Exchequer (No. 11) and that of the Chief Whip (No. 12).

The Cenotaph *

Erected in 1919 to commemorate those whose lives were lost during World War I, the Cenotaph is the main focus of the Remembrance Sunday ceremony, which is held every November. A two-minute silence is observed for those who died in both World Wars.

Cabinet War Rooms **

Just down King Charles Street off Whitehall's west side are the **Cabinet War Rooms**, the underground headquarters of Churchill, the War Cabinet and Chiefs of Staff during World War II bombing raids. The complex includes Churchill's bedroom and study, a hospital, map room and shooting range. Open 10:00–18:00, daily.

Above: *The Old Admiralty faces on to the Horse Guards, the setting for the Trooping of the Colour.*
Below: *Colourful pageantry provides a free spectacle for visitors to the city.*

PARLIAMENT SQUARE

Laid out soon after the rebuilding of the Houses of
Parliament in the mid 1800s, Parliament Square is a
rather busy traffic roundabout and houses some of
London's most famous landmarks, such as the Houses of
Parliament, Big Ben and Westminster Abbey. There are
several interesting statues dotted about Parliament
Square, including those of Abraham Lincoln, Benjamin
Disraeli and a glowering Winston Churchill (in the
northeast corner of the green).

Houses of Parliament ★★★

The 'Mother of all Parliaments' is one of London's best-
known sights, a grandiose Victorian edifice on the north
bank of the Thames which has been the site of parlia-
mentary meetings since 1265. The 266m (872ft) riverside
façade is best appreciated from Westminster Bridge, or
the south bank of the Thames, with the ornate Victoria
Tower and its famous clock, which is known as **Big Ben**
rising up at its eastern end.

The House is divided into upper and lower houses,
the **House of Commons** and the **House of Lords**. A
wartime bomb destroyed the original Commons debating
chamber, and reconstruction was completed in 1950. On
the other side of the Central Lobby is the House of Lords,
a far more splendid chamber where debates are less
acrimonious and the atmosphere somewhat soporific.

Above: *Big Ben is the
largest clock in Britain.*
Right: *The Houses
of Parliament are an
impressive sight from
across the Thames.*

Facing Parliament Square on the north side of the House is **Westminster Hall**, the only surviving relic of the original palace. Across the road from the Houses of Parliament is the **Jewel Tower,** which houses an exhibition on parliament's history. Open daily 10:00–16:00.

Westminster Abbey ★★★

A masterpiece in its own right, the Abbey also presents a rich pageant of English history and has been the setting for almost every Coronation since 1066.

Built on the site of a monastery in the 11th century, the present church mostly dates from the 13th century and its soaring, 30m (98ft) nave is the loftiest in the country.

It would take a whole book to describe the hundreds of memorials which fill the Abbey, but the highlights include the Tomb of the Unknown Warrior (representing British troops who died in World War I), the Perpendicular Henry VII Chapel, the Coronation Chair, the Royal Chapels, Statesman's Corner and Poet's Corner.

The Tate Gallery ★★★

A short walk from Parliament Square is the Tate Gallery, situated on Millbank. This holds a vast collection of historic and contemporary paintings and sculptures from both Britain and overseas, including the Turner collection (some 282 paintings and 20,000 drawings). The Tate has a reputation for innovative, controversial exhibits of contemporary works, but there are also plenty of old favourites on display. Open 10:00–17:50, daily. The Tate Gallery of Modern Art is due to open in what was Bankside Power Station in 2000.

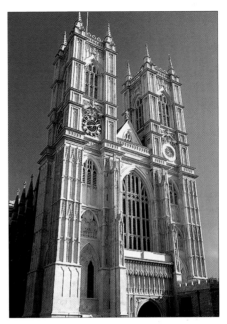

Above: *Westminster Abbey contains the tombs of many medieval monarchs.*

EXPLORING THE ABBEY

There is a charge to visit the Abbey, and the entrance is via the north Transept (expect queues in summer). Open 09:20–16:45 Mon–Fri, 09:20–14:45 Sat. Audio guides are available, and guided tours are offered by the Abbey's vergers. For details and bookings phone (0171) 222-7110. There is a separate charge to visit the Chapter House and Museum, open 10:30–16:00 daily.

Above: *Buckingham Palace is a 'must' on every tourist itinerary.*
Opposite: *St James's Park is one of the great London parks, where you can relax on a deckchair listening to the band, feed the ducks or take a leisurely stroll.*

NASH AND THE PALACE

Buckingham House, which originally stood on this site, was the home of the Duke of Buckingham until 1762 when it was sold to George III. His successor, George IV, commissioned his favourite architect (John Nash) to expand and overhaul the house, but it wasn't until the 19-year-old Queen Victoria acceded to the throne in 1837 that it became the official Royal Palace. Nash had placed a triumphal arch in front of the palace but in 1851 this was moved to its present site in Hyde Park and is now called the Marble Arch.

ROYAL LONDON
Buckingham Palace ★★★

The official London residence of the monarch since Queen Victoria's reign, Buckingham Palace is a vast monolith (usually surrounded by throngs of tourists) which impresses by virtue of its size rather than by any architectural graces it may possess.

Apart from those select few who are invited to the Queen's annual garden parties, the Palace has only been open to the public since 1993, when it was decided to admit visitors to help defray the costs of re-building Windsor Castle after a disastrous fire (*see* p. 112–13). The Palace is only accessible during August and September (open 09:30–16:30, daily) when the Queen and her family are at their summer retreat in Balmoral.

The tour visits just 18 of the 600 rooms in the Palace, the most impressive being the richly decorated Throne Room, the State Dining Room, the Blue Drawing Room and the Music Room. You can also visit the **Queen's Gallery**, where regularly changing exhibitions from one of the greatest private art collections in the world are on display throughout the year (open 09:30–16:30, daily).

Further down Buckingham Palace Road you can visit the working stables of the **Royal Mews** (open 12:00–16:00, Tues, Wed, Thur; 10:30–17:00, Mon–Thur, Aug and Sept). The original Kings Mews were pulled down to make way for Trafalgar Square, and both the new mews and Trafalgar Square were designed by **John Nash**, who was commissioned by the Prince Regent (later crowned George IV). The main attractions of the mews are the magnificent gilded and polished state carriages and coaches, which have been used for every Royal Coronation since 1831.

The Mall *

This broad, tree-lined boulevard sweeps down from the **Victoria Memorial** outside Buckingham Palace to the enormous **Admiralty Arch**, which frames the southwest corner of Trafalgar Square.

To the south of the Mall is **St James's Park**, created as a hunting reserve by Henry VIII and first opened to the public by Charles II, who liked to walk here with his mistress. The attractive lake in the park is home to ducks and Canada geese.

On the north side of the Mall at the Buckingham Palace end is **Lancaster House** and **Clarence House** (neither is open to public viewing; the latter is the home of the Queen Mother). A little further east lies **St James's Palace**, which was the sovereign's residence prior to the reconstruction of Buckingham Palace, and which now provides a London home for the Prince of Wales.

Adjacent to it is the **Chapel Royal**, which can be viewed during services (08:15 and 11:15 on Sundays, October–April only).

Past **Marlborough House** (designed by Wren) is the impressive façade of Carlton House Terrace, built by John Nash under the patronage of George IV.

From the **Duke of York's Steps** in the middle of the terrace there are views across St James's Park, and to the east of the steps is the entrance to the **Institute of Contemporary Art,** or ICA, a trendy hangout for London's avant-garde set. The ICA has a regular and varied programme of films, talks, exhibitions and other events. The ICA Gallery is open 12:00–19:30, daily.

As one of London's largest squares, Trafalgar Square has been at the centre of both political demonstrations and public revelry ever since it was created. The Chartists (campaigning for reform of the voting laws) marched from here in 1848, and in 1936 the Jarrow Crusade (on a 'hunger march' from a ship-building town in the northeast of England) finished their 300 mile walk in the square.

Huge anti-nuclear demonstrations were held here in the 1980s, and a constant vigil was maintained outside South Africa House until the end of the apartheid era in the early 90s. On a more celebratory note, the relief of Mafeking was marked on 17 May 1900 by drunken crowds thronging the square, and every New Year's Eve the square plays host to massive (and mostly inebriated) crowds heralding the New Year.

Below: *Nelson gazes out from the top of his column in Trafalgar Square.*

TRAFALGAR SQUARE

The largest public area in London, Trafalgar Square formed part of architect John Nash's grand designs to transform the city in the mid-19th century. The square was named after Nelson's famous naval victory over the French in 1805, and the 52m (170ft) **Nelson's Column** – the focal point of the square – was finished in 1843, as was the National Gallery on its north side. The famous lions at the base of the column were added in 1867, but the fountains were not installed until 1936, nearly 70 years later.

On the west side of the square is the neoclassical Canada House (originally the Royal College of Physicians), whose Portland Stone façade is echoed on the east side by the South Africa House. The best view over Trafalgar Square is from the steps of the National Gallery, looking down past Nelson's Column and along the length of Whitehall to Big Ben beyond.

Tucked into the northeast corner of the square is **St Martin-in-the-Fields**, built in 1726. It has a fine Corinthian portico, topped by an unusual tower and steeple, and the interior boasts an Italian plasterwork ceiling. There's a small craft and clothes market outside the church, and the crypt houses a brass-rubbing centre.

In December the square is lit up by an enormous, beautifully decorated Christmas tree. A new tree is donated annually by Norway in thanks to Britain for its role in the country's liberation from the Nazis during World War II.

The National Gallery ★★★

Housing one of the world's greatest permanent art collections, the National Gallery contains over 2000 paintings, including famous works of the Old Masters. The collection was begun as late as 1824 with only a few pieces, but today the scope – spanning Western Art from 1260 to 1900 – is so enormous that it is impossible to absorb it all in one go. If you are pressed for time, the *20 Great Paintings* booklet (obtainable at the Gallery) will prove helpful. The gallery was given a new lease of life with the opening of the five-storey Sainsbury Wing (funded by the supermarket chain) in 1991, which houses the Early Renaissance Collection. If you want to peruse the paintings chronologically, the Sainsbury Wing is the place to start. Open 10:00–18:00 Monday–Saturday (Wednesday until 20:00); 12:00–18:00, Sunday.

The National Portrait Gallery ★★

Founded in 1856, the National Portrait Gallery houses some 10,000 portraits (including paintings, drawings, sculptures and photographs) of famous men and women from the Middle Ages to the present day. From politicians to poets, and from royalty to pop stars, there is something for everyone to enjoy in this entertaining collection. It starts with the Tudors on the top floor, working down to post-war personalities on ground floor level. The Gallery houses the only known portrait of William Shakespeare. Open 10:00–18:00, Monday–Saturday; 12:00–18:00, Sunday.

THE NATIONAL GALLERY

The majority of the capital's modern and British collections of art are found in the Tate Gallery (*see* p. 39), while the main strengths of the **National Gallery** are in early Renaissance Italian, Dutch, and 17th-century Spanish paintings. Some of the star attractions include the **Leonardo Cartoon** (chalk drawing of the Virgin and Child with St John the Baptist, 1510); the **Baptism of Christ** by Piero della Francesca (a pioneer of early Renaissance perspective, 1450); the **Rokeby Venus** by Diego Velázquez (1649); John Constable's **Haywain** (classic portrayal of the English countryside, 1821) and Hans Holbein's **The Ambassadors** (1533).

Opposite above:
The National Gallery and St Martin-in-the-Fields on the north side of Trafalgar Square.
Left: *Trafalgar Square at Christmas. The giant Christmas tree is an annual gift from Norway.*

3
The West End

Although it is situated in the heart of the city, the West End acquired its name during the 19th century, when this area, west of the original commercial centre, became a desirable residential district, and smart shops and upmarket hotels established themselves among the city's formal squares and mews terraces. Today the West End is the capital's principal shopping and entertainment district.

London's major theatres and cinemas are concentrated around **Leicester Square** and **Piccadilly Circus**, which form part of **Soho**. Traditionally, Soho has been home to immigrants from Irish, Israeli, Italian, Chinese and even Huguenot descent. The invention of the laundromat forced the Chinese to diversify from traditional laundry businesses in the East End to restaurant ownership. **Chinatown** is now one of the best-known areas in which to enjoy a cheap meal after the theatre or cinema.

Soho's bohemian atmosphere has always attracted writers, artists and musicians, and, more recently, media folk. Its dual personality is evident in the existence of porn shops alongside smart clubs and trendy shops. It was largely to distance the up-and-coming area around Mayfair from the relative squalor of Soho that **Regent Street** was laid out in the early 1800s, when over 700 houses and small shops were demolished to make way for Nash's grand design. Today Regent Street and **Bond Street** are among the capital's classiest shopping streets. Nearby Savile Row is famed as the home of bespoke English tailoring. **Oxford Street**, to the north, provides a vast range of shops along its busy length.

DON'T MISS

*** Soho:** soak up the bohemian atmosphere.
** Piccadilly:** English tea at the **Ritz** or **Fortnum's**.
** Charing Cross Road:** browse in the bookshops and peruse the exhibitions at the **Photographer's Gallery**.
** Piccadilly Circus:** see it by night, followed by a show at a top West End theatre.
** Bond Street** and **Regent Street:** window-shopping in the exclusive stores.
* Chinatown:** explore exotic supermarkets and try some great food in Soho.

Opposite: *Regent Street curves to the north from busy Piccadilly Circus.*

Above: *Soho has changed its image in recent years, although night-time entertainment is still one of the main attractions.*

SOHO

One of the city's most colourful areas, Soho buzzes with activity 24 hours a day, particularly by night. Once London's principal red-light district, it has been cleaned up in recent years (although strip joints, including the famous Raymond Revuebar, still operate) and now offers a vast range of fashionable cafés, brasseries, restaurants, discos, clubs and, of course, cinemas and theatres.

Shaftesbury Avenue is one of the main theatre areas, and also has a few cinemas and clubs (such as the famous Limelight Club). Parallel to Shaftesbury Avenue, **Old Compton Street** is typical of the peculiar mixture which characterizes Soho, with sex shops rubbing shoulders with Continental patisseries and cafés, fashion boutiques, gay bars, trendy brasseries and specialized food shops.

There are many interesting little corners to be discovered while wandering around the network of streets in this vicinity. **Frith Street** has a plaque on the house where Mozart once stayed, and it was in a room above a restaurant here that John Logie Baird gave the first ever public demonstration of his new invention, the television, in 1926. Ronnie Scott's famous jazz club was founded here in 1958. **Dean Street** boasts a plaque to Karl Marx, and the **Ben Uri Gallery** (open 10:00–17:00, Monday–Thursday; 14:00–17:00, Sunday) focuses on contemporary Jewish art. Soho's vice rackets are mostly concentrated to the west of **Wardour Street**, where you will also find the colourful (and cheap) **Berwick Street Market**.

Charing Cross Road *

Dividing Soho from Covent Garden to the east, Charing Cross Road boasts several theatres and the highest concentration of bookshops in the city. Other than the

---

HALF-PRICE THEATRE

On the south side of Leicester Square, the Society of West End Theatres operates a **ticket booth** where you can get seats at half-price for any West End show for that day's performance. It's open from noon for matinees, and 14:30–18:30 for evening performances. If they've sold out for a particular show you'd set your heart on seeing, try booking agencies such as First Call, tel: (0171) 497-9977 or Ticketmaster, tel: (0171) 344-4000. Premium prices are, of course, charged for popular musicals and long-running hits.

rambling expanses of Foyle's and Waterstone's there are numerous specialist and second-hand bookshops, particularly in **Cecil Court** below Leicester Square tube station. Nearby is the excellent **Photographer's Gallery** which has interesting (and free) exhibitions. Open 11:00–19:00, Tuesday–Saturday.

Leicester Square *

Adjoining Charing Cross Road, Leicester Square is where all the big movies are premiered and it also has several popular clubs and discos at its fringes. The gardens at the centre of the square (a notorious hangout for junkies in days gone by) feature busts of artists and writers and a statue of Charlie Chaplin, with the useful Society of West End Theatres booth on the south side (see p. 42).

Chinatown *

To the north of Leicester Square is Chinatown, a small enclave focused around Gerrard Street with its red-and-gold gateways and pagoda-style telephone boxes. Chinese supermarkets and ornament shops co-exist alongside numerous restaurants, open late into the night, where you can find everything from Cantonese cuisine to crispy duck. The restaurants here (particularly the smaller ones which look more like cafés) are usually reasonably priced, and full to overflowing on Sundays with Chinese families tucking into their **dim sum**.

> ### CHINESE NEW YEAR
>
> If you're in the city for the **Chinese New Year** (late Jan or early Feb) head down to **Gerrard Street** to witness one of the noisiest celebrations in the capital, with firecrackers exploding everywhere as colourful papier-mâché lions dance through Chinatown trying to grab the cabbages, decorated with bank notes, which residents hang from their windows. This exuberant event attracts Chinese people, as well as sightseers, from all over London.

Left: *Chinese New Year is a colourful and joyous celebration when Chinatown comes alive with dragons and parades.*

PICCADILLY AND REGENT STREET
Piccadilly Circus ★

Originally known as Regent Circus and forming part of Nash's grand plan for Regent Street, Piccadilly Circus is one of the main hubs of the West End and a popular tourist spot – although Londoners are more likely to curse the traffic or pedestrian congestion and wonder what on earth everybody is doing here.

Trocadero ★★

One of the main attractions of Piccadilly Circus, apart from the statue of **Eros**, is the three-storey Trocadero complex, with its fascinating shops and several hi-tech interactive entertainment centres featuring the latest in electronic wizardry.

Piccadilly is no stranger to outlandish entertainment: in the 1830s the **Egyptian Hall** displayed Siamese twins, the 2ft-high 'General' Tom Thumb, and a mermaid (half-monkey, half-fish), among other curiosities. The 1990s equivalents include the chance to participate in **Segaworld** with its hi-tech simulated rides; the 40-metre **Troc Drop**, the world's first indoor free-fall ride; the **Emaginator,** a back-jolting ride accompanied by 'motion simulation' films; **Funland,** with an assortment of various computer games and virtual reality simulations, and the **Pepsi Imax 3D Cinema**, which shows 2D and 3D films on a screen five storeys high and **Planet Hollywood**. The centre is open 10:00–24:00 daily.

Below: *Piccadilly Circus, lit by vast neon hoardings.*

Next door to the Trocadero in the old London Pavilion music hall is Madame Tussaud's **Rock Circus,** where 'moving' waxwork figures 'mime' sound- tracks which are played on personal head-phones as you travel down the historical road of rock 'n roll. Open 11:00– 21:00, Mon, Wed, Thurs and Sun; 12:00– 21:00, Tues; 11:00–22:00, Fri and Sat.

Regent Street **

Curving northwards from Piccadilly Circus towards Oxford Street, Regent Street is one of the West End's prime shopping zones, with many well-known shops such as Hamleys (the world's largest toy shop), Aquascutum (classic men's clothing); Garrards (the Queen's jewellers), Dickins & Jones (fashion and beauty) and Liberty's (which has an interesting mock-Tudor

façade on its north side). At the southern end of Regent Street, the **Café Royal** was a popular hangout with writers and artists (including Oscar Wilde, George Bernard Shaw and Aubrey Beardsley at the beginning of the century, and still retains an air of faded grandeur.

Behind Regent Street and to the east is **Carnaby Street**, once a focal point (with the King's Road) of the 'Swinging Sixties', but now a cheap shopping area.

Piccadilly **

Leading from Piccadilly Circus down to Hyde Park Corner, **Piccadilly** itself is a busy road where you can take afternoon tea at famous establishments such as the **Ritz Hotel** or **Fortnum and Mason**, the epicurean emporium which supplies delicacies to the Royal household, and magnificent picnic hampers for society events.

Above: *The Tudor-style façade of Liberty's, one of London's most exclusive department stores and famous for its fabric designs.*
Below: *The luxurious Fortnum and Mason where you may, among other things, purchase many varieties of tea and other traditional English fare in the ground-floor food hall.*

Behind Fortnum and Mason, there is a small enclave between Piccadilly and the Mall, which has been a fashionable haunt since Henry VIII built St James's Palace in the 1530s, with courtiers and pillars of society disporting themselves ever since in its smart shops and exclusive clubs.

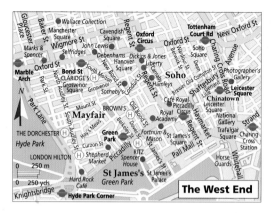

The West End

At the heart of this exclusive area is **St James's Square**, laid out in the 1670s. Some houses here have seen a succession of illustrious residents: No. 10 was home to prime ministers Pitt the Elder, Lord Derby and Gladstone (today it houses the offices of the prestigious Royal Institute for International Affairs). No. 4 was the home of Nancy Astor, who became the first female MP to sit in the House of Commons in 1919. During World War II, both General Eisenhower and General de Gaulle had headquarters here. At No. 14 is the **London Library**, a private lending library founded by historian Thomas Carlyle.

To the west of St James's Square can be found the auctioneers, **Christie's**, while just to the south is the unusual **Schomberg House**, with a 17th-century red brick façade; the painter Gainsborough lived here in the last years of his life.

To the north of St James's Square and running parallel with Piccadilly is **Jermyn Street**, one of London's most elegant shopping streets. Among the windows worth peering in at along here are those of Davidoff (cigars), Turnbull & Asser (shirts), Floris (perfumes), and Bates (hatters). On the corner with Duke Street is the **Pipe Smokers' Museum** within the Dunhill shop. Inside, pipes of every shape and description are displayed. Open 10:00–16:00, Monday–Saturday.

In St James's Place is Spencer House, a splendid 18th century town house built for the first Earl of Spencer, ancestor of the late Diana, Princess of Wales. In the 1980s Lord Rothschild restored it to its original magnificence, and guided tours are available 10:45–16:45 on Sundays (closed January and August).

On Piccadilly itself is **St James's Church**, built by Wren

Opposite: *The Burlington Arcade, built in the 19th century, houses many small and exclusive shops.* **Below:** *The doorman outside Fortnum and Mason. The store is renowned for its elegance and prestige.*

in 1684 and said to have been his favourite amongst the many London churches he was responsible for. Although much altered since then (partly due to bomb damage in 1940), it still features an airy, graceful interior and an ornate altar screen carved by the 17th-century master Grinling Gibbons; the organ was moved here from the chapel at the Whitehall Palace in 1691. William Blake and Pitt the Elder were baptised in this church, which today hosts society weddings, lectures, and concerts as well as ministering to the homeless and running a daily craft market and vegetarian café.

Gentlemen's Clubs *

Pall Mall and St James's Street are famous for their private clubs, many of which still traditionally exclude women. Most were founded in the early 19th century. The oldest is **White's** (with a membership which includes Prince Charles, top politicians, and military brass), while the **Carlton Club** is favoured by top Tories and the **Reform Club** was traditionally the home of the liberals.

The Burlington Arcade **

On the other side of Piccadilly is the superb Regency Mall known as the Burlington Arcade, with delightful, old-fashioned mahogany-fronted shops selling smart shirts, luggage, jewellery and other expensive items. Next door, Burlington House is home to the **Royal Academy**. Founded in 1768, it holds several exhibitions annually, including the well-known Summer Exhibition. Open 10:00–18:00, daily.

If you walk through the Burlington Arcade you will come to what was until 1997 the Museum of Mankind. It contained the ethnographic collections of the British Museum, where they will be displayed once the redevelopment is complete (*see* p. 53). Almost opposite is **Savile Row**, the home of some of Britain's most exclusive tailors.

(*see* p. 53)

CHRISTMAS LIGHTS

During the pre-Christmas rush there is no busier place than Oxford Street and the surrounding area, with traffic wardens continually marshalling shoppers to stop them from blocking the roads or falling under the wheels of a bus. Most are probably busy gawking at the famous **Christmas lights** which adorn the streets from mid-November onwards. Oxford Street, Regent Street and Bond Street usually all have **lighting up ceremonies** where celebrities throw the switches, and various jollities are provided, including carol singers, horse-drawn carriages, choirs, musicians, seasonal refreshments and, of course, late-night shopping. Contact the Tourist Board (*see* Tourist Information, p.122) for exact dates.

Above: *Shepherd Market is a popular spot for al fresco eating during the summer.*

MAYFAIR AND OXFORD STREET

Mayfair *

Situated to the north of Piccadilly, Mayfair is one of the most upmarket residential areas in London. It is an aristocratic enclave where major landowners such as the Berkeleys and Grosvenors built grand squares (which still bear their names) surrounded by palatial mansions in the middle of the 18th century. Embassies, consulates and swish hotels (such as Claridges) now predominate, with some of the city's top shopping districts, clubs and casinos (in St James's and Curzon Street respectively) within convenient reach.

Mayfair is bordered on the west by **Park Lane**, where luxury hotels such as the Dorchester and Hilton enjoy views over Hyde Park.

Shepherd Market *

Between Mayfair and Piccadilly lies a maze of alleys and passageways, which still retain a village-like atmosphere. Here you will find a number of fashionable restaurants and pubs, from which people overflow onto the pavements in summer.

Bond Street **

Cutting right through the heart of Mayfair, Bond Street (divided into New Bond Street in the north and Old Bond Street in the south) harbours some of the most

---

A DAY AT SELFRIDGES

One of the great landmarks of Oxford Street is the imposing, colonnaded façade of **Selfridges**, which opened in 1909, just four years after Harrods in Knightsbridge, and challenged the latter's dominance by marketing itself as being 'dedicated to the service of women'. 'Why not spend a day at Selfridges?' was the novel theme promoted by its owner, Chicago millionaire Gordon Selfridge. The store houses 130 departments. One of its original Art Deco lifts is now in the Museum of London (*see* p. 74).

Left: *The Hard Rock Cafe is one of London's most popular eating places and something of an institution, having recently celebrated its 25th anniversary.*
Below: *One of London's most famous shops, Asprey's on Bond Street is a luxurious choice if you are shopping for jewellery, silver, china or other exclusive gift items.*

exclusive and expensive shops in London: Chanel, Asprey's, Cartier, Versace and Hermes are all found along here. Bond Street is also noted for its fine art galleries, and its resident auctioneers, Sotheby's.

Oxford Street *

Perhaps one of London's best-known shopping areas, Oxford Street was developed as long ago as the 1780s to cater for the wealthy residents who were then moving out of the old city centre into more fashionable areas in the West End. This 2km (1 mile) street is still one of the world's most profitable retailing districts despite numerous recessions and very high rents. There are also several good quality department stores such as Selfridges, Marks & Spencer, John Lewis, C&A and Debenhams.

Off Oxford Street to the north of Manchester Square is the **Wallace Collection** in Hertford House (open 10:00–17:00, Monday–Saturday; 14:00–17:00, Sunday), which offers a fabulous display of European art (particularly 18th century works), and an impressive armoury.

ERECTED BY JOHN DUKE OF BEDFORD 1830

4
Bloomsbury and Covent Garden

A stone's throw from the busy shops of Oxford Street and adjacent Tottenham Court Road (the main centre for hi-fi and computer retailing in London), **Bloomsbury** is, by contrast, a low-key area known for its many pleasant public squares and literary associations. Home to London University, University College Hospital and numerous book publishers, the area was also the birthplace of the famous Bloomsbury Group during the inter-war years, an intellectual circle of friends that included Virginia Woolf, D H Lawrence, Bertrand Russell, E M Forster and Rupert Brooke. Today the main attraction in the area is the **British Museum**, a venerable institution which is about to undergo a major transformation: London's first covered square – and one of its most imaginative public spaces – is to be created at the heart of this historic museum.

To the south of Bloomsbury, High Holborn leads to the tranquil legal enclaves of the historical buildings of the **Inns of Court**, the main centre of jurisprudence in the city for the last 700 years.

One of the liveliest areas of central London, **Covent Garden** was once the capital's main market for fruit, flowers and vegetables until the wholesale market was moved out to a purpose-built complex south of the Thames near Battersea in 1974. In the last two decades it has been redeveloped and has gradually blossomed as a tourist attraction in its own right, bursting with trendy wine bars and restaurants, smart clothes shops, arts and crafts markets and almost non-stop street entertainment.

DON'T MISS

*** British Museum: outstanding collections. Follow it with a stroll around Bloomsbury's leafy squares and a visit to **Dickens' House**.
*** Covent Garden: markets, shops and restaurants of this trendy area.
** Courtauld Galleries: Impressionist and Post-Impressionist collections.
** Sir John Soane's Museum: eclectic collections in Holborn.

Opposite: *Covent Garden's market hall, built in the 1830s, was London's produce market for over 100 years.*

BLOOMSBURY

This area has a pleasant architectural coherence, and its leafy, Georgian squares (among them **Russell Square**, **Bedford Square**, **Gordon Square**, and **Tavistock Square**) provide a tranquil and welcome respite from the hubbub of city life in London. On the eastern fringes of Bloomsbury is **Dickens' House** which is in fact only one of 15 houses that the novelist occupied in London. The interior boasts letters, pictures, manuscripts, and original furniture from Dickens' time, giving an interesting insight into the writer's personal and professional life. Open 10:00–17:00, Monday–Saturday.

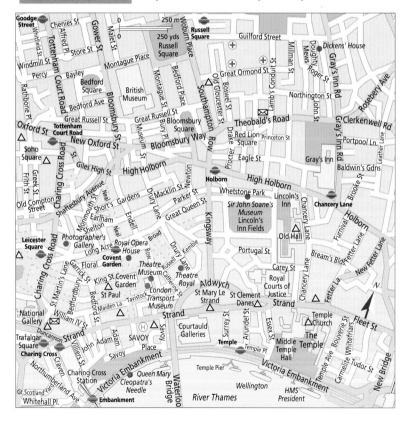

Left: *The British Museum's collections were largely built up in the days of the Empire.*

British Museum ★★★

The British Museum never fails to astound one but, given its size, plan for more than one visit. The extraordinary collections span from prehistoric times to the present day. Founded in the late 18th century, the museum has over four million exhibits in 94 galleries – a walk through all of them would cover 4km (2½ miles) – and is one of the most popular tourist attractions in the country, with around six million visitors annually.

The museum's great strengths are its collections of treasures and artworks from ancient Egypt, Greece and Rome, as well as Asia and the Far East, in addition to superb treasures from Roman and Anglo-Saxon Britain.

It's impossible to digest it all at once, and you might like to opt for one of the guided tours (four daily weekdays, three on Sundays), which cover many of the highlights. Open 10:00–17:00, Monday–Saturday; 12:00–18:00, Sunday. For bookings, tel: (0171) 323-8599.

Treasures include the Rosetta Stone (dating from 196BC, it unlocked the language of ancient Egypt), mummies of the Pharaohs in the Egyptian Galleries; the human-headed lions and bulls of ancient Assyria; the Elgin Marbles and other Greek masterpieces; the Portland Vase with its exquisitely carved blue and white glass;. the Lindow Man (sacrificed during a Druidic ceremony, his well-preserved body was found in peat in 1984), and the Sutton Hoo Anglo-Saxon treasures.

THE GREAT COURT

As the millennium approaches, the British Museum is about to undergo a remarkable transformation which will result in the creation of London's first covered square - and one of its most imaginative public spaces – at its heart. Since its inception the museum has also been home to the **British Library** but due to lack of space the Library is now moving to a new (and much derided) building next to St Pancras Station. The famous **Round Reading Room** (where Marx, Lenin and many other luminaries have studied) will become accessible to the general public for the first time in its history, as will the **Great Court** in which it stands (this has not been seen by the public since 1857 when it was filled up with book stacks). Under a vast, translucent roof, the Great Court will also house a new, multi-level cultural complex.

Right: *Covent Garden is always alive with street entertainers and musicians of all kinds.*
Opposite: *A fashionable part of London popular with tourists and Londoners alike, Covent Garden offers a wide choice of restaurants, cafés and wine bars.*

LONDON'S FIRST POLICE FORCE

The licentiousness of Covent Garden during the 18th century, with its thinly-disguised brothels and bawdy houses, led to the formation of the nation's first police force. A magistrate's court had been established in Bow Street in 1748 and two resident magistrates, Henry Fielding (author of *Tom Jones*) and his brother John, set up their own private force of six plain-clothes policemen who became known as the **Bow Street Runners**. Although they had some success in cleaning up prostitution, lawlessness still ruled: in 1770, the Prime Minister, Lord Chancellor and Prince of Wales were all robbed in broad daylight in the West End. Mounted patrols operated from Bow Street from 1805, but it wasn't until 1829 that a unified force, the Metropolitan Police, was finally created.

COVENT GARDEN

At the core of Covent Garden is the **piazza** – London's oldest planned square – which was originally designed by Inigo Jones in the 1630s. It was a very desirable residential area until market traders started moving in, and later, insalubrious coffee houses, gambling dens and brothels sprang up around the piazza. The central **market hall** was built in the 1830s (the glass roof was added later) and continued to be the country's most important wholesale fruit and vegetable market until it was relocated to Vauxhall in 1974. Today the market hall, piazza and surrounding streets (particularly in the converted warehouses to the north) are crammed with speciality shops, restaurants, pubs and much more besides. It has become one of London's major tourist attractions. On the west side of the piazza is **St Paul's Church** – known as the 'Actors' Church' due to its proximity to theatreland – which has numerous memorials to famous actors and actresses. Appropriately enough, the space in front of the church is now the main venue for Covent Garden's **street entertainers**, with an almost non-stop parade of jugglers, mime artists, breakdancers and buskers every day and night.

Facing Bow Street on the east side of the piazza is the **Royal Opera House**, home to the Royal Ballet and Opera. Built in the early 19th century, this grandiose building is currently undergoing major redevelopment.

London Transport Museum **

One of the old market sheds on the east side houses the museum which traces the history of transport in the capital from old horse-drawn buses to trams, the underground (the world's oldest, begun in 1863), buses and much more. There are plenty of interactive exhibits (including a computer-simulated tube-train drive) and a section on the Underground's famous poster collection. Open Saturday–Thursday 10:00–18:00; Friday 11:00–18:00.

Theatre Museum **

Round the corner in Russell Street is the Theatre Museum (open 11:00–19:00, Tuesday–Sunday) which contains memorabilia including theatre props, programmes and costumes from the world of ballet, theatre, circus and opera. There's also a semi-permanent display ('Slap'), of the history of stage make-up. Demonstrations are given six times daily (between 11:15 and 17:00), and you may be the person picked from the audience for a theatrical face make-up. Nearby, in the Covent Garden piazza, the **Cabaret Mechanical Theatre** houses a collection of around 40–50 push-button machines, bizarre inventions, and entertaining automated gadgets. Open 09:30–18:30 daily.

Theatre Royal, Drury Lane *

This was one of the first theatres to be built in London after the end of Oliver Cromwell's puritanical rule (during which theatre-going was banned), and was completed in 1663. After a fire it was rebuilt in 1812, and re-modelled again in 1921. The staircases and foyer feature an impressive range of statues and paintings of famous actors. You can join an interesting tour (three times daily, tel: (0171) 494-5091 for bookings) which covers the theatre's history, the Royal Box, back-stage and even beneath the stage. The theatre is known as Theatre Royal, Drury Lane even though the entrance is on Catherine Street.

> **MARKETS AND SHOPS**
>
> The main market at Covent Garden is in the central **market hall**, mostly specializing in arts and crafts, but don't expect too many bargains. On the south side of the piazza the **Jubilee Hall market** offers mainly clothes and accessories. Stalls rotate regularly and on Mondays both areas feature antiques. In King Street is the Africa Craft Centre which also has a restaurant. Some of the most interesting shops are found in the area just to the north of the main piazza, principally in **Floral Street**, **Long Acre**, and **Neal Street**. Just off Short's Gardens, **Neal's Yard** is the main focal point for 'alternative' culture in the area, with a wholefood shop, excellent vegetarian cafés, bakeries and a herbal centre. Neal's Yard Dairy specializes in British cheeses.

CLEOPATRA'S NEEDLE

This 18m (59ft) obelisk was originally one of a pair from Cleopatra's Palace outside Alexandria, and dates back nearly 3500 years. It was presented to Britain by Egypt's ruler in 1819, but it took another 60 years before it was finally erected on this spot – and even then the sphinxes which flank it were placed back to front. A wit of the day coined the following ditty:

> 'This monument,
> as some supposes,
> Was looked upon
> of old by Moses.
> It passed in time
> from Greek to Turks
> And was stuck up here
> by the Board of Works.'

THE STRAND

Connecting Trafalgar Square with Fleet Street, the **Strand** was once on the waterfront, and in the late 19th century it was at the heart of London's theatreland. One of the few theatres left is the **Adelphi Theatre**, built in 1806 and re-modelled in Art Deco style in the 1930s. On the south side of the Strand is the **Savoy Theatre**, adjoining the famous Savoy Hotel. Opened in 1889, the Savoy is one of the city's grandest hotels and its forecourt is the only street in the UK where traffic drives on the right. The impressive Art Deco **Thames Foyer** is well worth seeing; you can also enjoy a proper English tea in these elegant surroundings.

The Courtauld Galleries ★★★

Just down from the Savoy is **Somerset House**, an imposing classical building set around a courtyard. Built in 1786 on the site of the palace of the Earls of Somerset, it was the first major building in the country to be designed as offices. One wing, originally built for the Royal Academy of Arts, is now home to the Courtauld Galleries (open 10:00–18:00, Monday–Saturday; 14:00–18:00, Sunday) which house one of the finest collections of Impressionist and Post-Impressionist paintings in the country.

Below: *Splendid Art Deco features add allure to the grand Savoy Hotel.*

The galleries house works by Cézanne, Modigliani, Renoir, Gauguin and with some of the best-known paintings being Van Gogh's *Portrait of the Artist with a Bandaged Ear*, Manet's *Bar at the Folies Bergère*, and Degas' *Two Dancers*. Various artists from other periods (including Botticelli, Gainsborough and Rubens) are also represented.

Victoria Embankment ★

Parallel to the Strand along the banks of the Thames, the Victoria Embankment was the first London thoroughfare to be lit by electricity (in 1879). Between Waterloo and Hungerford bridges on the Embankment are the Victoria Embankment Gardens, which house a statue of Scottish bard Robert Burns, and feature concerts on the lawn during summer. On the other side of the road is **Cleopatra's Needle**, London's oldest monument.

The Inns of Court *

Close to Bloomsbury and Covent Garden is the area which has been the focal point of the country's legal system since the 13th century. Here, potential lawyers studied, ate and slept at one of the four **Inns of Court** (Gray's Inn, Lincoln's Inn, Middle Temple and Inner Temple), and vestiges of this 'live-in' system of learning still persist today; barristers are required to eat a specified number of dinners here before they can qualify to practise at the Bar.

Above: Middle Temple Hall has a splendid Elizabethan hammerbeam roof and was the setting for the first performance of William Shakespeare's Twelfth Night *in 1602.*

Some of the more interesting buildings to explore include the **Middle Temple Hall** (open 10:00–11:30 and 15:00–16:30, Monday–Friday) whose wood-panelled walls date from the 16th century and are hung with portraits of Tudor kings and queens; **Temple Church** (open 10:00–16:00, Wednesday–Sunday) which was built in 1185 by the Knights Templars, and features stone effigies of the Crusaders.

Sir John Soane's Museum **

On the north side of Lincoln's Inn Fields, this museum is one of London's best kept secrets. Based on the personal accumulation of art works and antiques of architect Sir John Soane, this unusual collection includes works by Hogarth, Reynolds, Turner and Canaletto, and many of his architectural drawings. In the basement of this intriguing house is the Egyptian sarcophagus of Seti I. Open 10:00–17:00, Tuesday–Saturday.

OLD CURIOSITY SHOP

Just to the south of Lincoln's Inn Fields at 13–14 Portsmouth Street, the **Old Curiosity Shop** is unlikely to have been the original shop for Charles Dickens' famous story of the same name. However, it is a genuine 17th-century building with a typical overhanging first floor and almost certainly one of the oldest shops in central London.

5
West and Southwest London

Separated from Notting Hill and Bayswater by the green expanse of Hyde Park, the Royal Borough of **Kensington** still has an air of exclusivity about it, although it is no longer the aristocratic suburb it was over 100 years ago. **Kensington Palace**, a royal residence, adjoins **Kensington Gardens** and **Hyde Park**, which together form London's largest park. To the south, **Knightsbridge** is a smart residential area – the famous **Harrods** store is its main attraction.

Several of London's top museums are located in **South Kensington** ('South Ken' to Londoners), with the **Victoria and Albert**, **Natural History** and **Science museums** next door to each other. These are the legacy of the 1851 **Great Exhibition of the Works of Industry of All Nations**, keenly promoted by Prince Albert, Queen Victoria's consort. It featured a unique wrought-iron and glass 'Crystal Palace' as its centrepiece, filled with exhibits from around the world. On the southern side of Hyde Park, the Crystal Palace drew over six million visitors and the Exhibition's profits were used to buy 35ha (87 acres) of land nearby to create a 'Museumland' to promote the arts and sciences. This led to the creation of South Kensington's museums. The palace was torn down and reconstructed in southeast London, where it burned down in 1936.

Neighbouring **Chelsea** features many tranquil mews houses and prime residential streets such as Cheyne Walk on the banks of the Thames, but its best-known thoroughfare is **King's Road**, birthplace of the 'Swinging Sixties', and still one of London's fashion Meccas.

DON'T MISS

*** **The museums of South Kensington:** particularly the new galleries at the **Natural History** and the **Science museums**, and the **Victoria and Albert Museum**.
*** **King's Road:** the fashion parade in trendy **Chelsea**.
** **Hyde Park:** walk, picnic, or jog – or hire a row boat on the Serpentine.
** **Notting Hill Carnival:** the exuberant carnival in August.
* **Knightsbridge:** window-shopping in **Harrods** and **Harvey Nichols**.

Opposite: *The richly decorated exterior of the Natural History Museum, which opened in 1881.*

NOTTING HILL AND BAYSWATER

To the north and northwest of Hyde Park respectively,
both Bayswater and Notting Hill are characterized by
the contrast of smart terraces and sweeping crescents
alongside rather down-at-heel areas, with similarly
cosmopolitan populations – in the case of Bayswater,
largely Arabic and Chinese communities, and in Notting
Hill mostly Afro-Caribbean.

London Toy and Model Museum ★

The main attraction in Bayswater is the huge London Toy
and Model Museum which can be found at 21 Craven
Hill. This excellent museum has recently been refurbished
and has now expanded to over 20 galleries on four floors.
It features beautifully displayed toys and models through
the centuries which will appeal to all children and adults.
Open 09:00–17:30 daily.

Notting Hill *

Notting Hill was one of the first areas in the capital (along with Brixton, Stockwell and Tottenham) to receive an influx of immigrants from the Caribbean in the post-war period, in this case primarily from Trinidad and Barbados. Already a poor slum area, it witnessed the country's first race riots in 1958 when competition for jobs and housing with white residents spilled over into violence. Partly to re-assert their Afro-Caribbean identity, the first **Notting Hill Carnival** was organized by the community in the early 1960s, based on the Trinidadian tradition of street carnivals. Held every August Bank Holiday, it is now Europe's biggest street festival, attracting upwards of a million spectators, and the largest carnival in the world apart from Rio.

The other main attraction in Notting Hill is the extensive **Portobello Road market** held every Saturday, featuring everything from antiques to clothing and even food, in an environment bursting with atmosphere.

HYDE PARK

London's largest park, Hyde Park was originally a hunting ground for Henry VIII, and was first opened to the public during the reign of James I. Together with adjoining Kensington Gardens it provides a massive open space (covering 250ha/618 acres) in the heart of the city, a haven for dog-walkers, joggers, horseriders, skateboarders and cyclists (as might be imagined, conflict between these different groups is common).

At the centre of the park is the **Serpentine**, a long, artificial lake popular for rowing (rowboats can be hired). There is also a swimming club at the Serpentine, and members pride themselves on swimming all through the year, especially

---

THE TYBURN GALLOWS

The corner of Hyde Park where the Marble Arch now stands was the site of the infamous **Tyburn Gallows** until they were demolished in 1825. The gallows (also known as the 'Tyburn Tree') coped with the execution of over 20 people at a time, and the almost daily hangings drew enormous crowds. In 1740, one guide book to London proclaimed it to be one of the city's chief attractions. The condemned were brought from Newgate Prison by cart, sometimes with the noose already in place, and allowed a free drink at ale houses along the way before being tied to the fatal tree; the cart was then whipped away. At the time, over 150 offences (including such minor misdemeanours as petty theft) warranted a one-way ticket to Tyburn.

Below: *Portobello Road is one of London's biggest and busiest antique markets.*

Right: *Horse riding is popular in Hyde Park along Rotten Row (the name is a corruption of* route du roi*).*
Below: *Speaker's Corner at Marble Arch, where anyone who wishes may address the crowds.*
Opposite: *The food hall at Harrods, in Knightsbridge, London's most famous department store where the emphasis is on quality and superb service.*

at Christmas. On the south side of the lake, the **Serpentine Gallery** holds interesting exhibitions, mostly of contemporary art. Open daily 10:00–18:00.

In Hyde Park's northeastern corner is **Marble Arch**, moved here in 1851 from outside Buckingham Palace. Until the end of the 18th century this was the site of the infamous Tyburn Gallows (*see* p. 61).

At present Marble Arch lies more or less stranded on a traffic island, but plans are afoot to redesign this junction at the west end of Oxford Street so that the arch is more accessible. Across from Marble Arch is **Speaker's Corner**, which has been a rallying point for political dissent since the 1850s, and is now best known for the soap-box orators who regularly entertain the crowds here (particularly on Sunday mornings) with their rantings and ravings.

Park Lane runs down the east side of the park, culminating in **Hyde Park Corner**, where **Constitution Arch** is also stranded in the middle of a busy traffic roundabout. On the north side of Hyde Park Corner is **Apsley House**, a remarkable mansion which was once the home of the Duke of Wellington (during his lifetime the house was referred to as Number One, London). Built by Robert Adam between 1771 and 1778, the house was occupied by the 'Iron Duke' when he was at the height of his career as the most powerful commander in Europe, and the lavish interior fittings, furnishings and paintings (which include works by Rubens, Velázquez, Goya and Correggio) reflect his stature at the time. Open 11:00–17:00, Tuesday–Sunday.

From Hyde Park Corner running past the southern edge of the Serpentine is **Rotten Row**, a fashionable bridlepath where the Household Cavalry exercise every morning from their nearby barracks. Past here is the **Albert Memorial**, opposite the **Royal Albert Hall** on Kensington Gore (*see* p. 67).

KNIGHTSBRIDGE

Knightsbridge and neighbouring Belgravia boast some of the priciest real estate in the capital, with numerous embassies and exclusive hotels scattered throughout their secluded squares. The main attraction for visitors, however, is **Harrods** – where you can buy anything from a loaf of bread to (reputedly) an elephant – on Brompton Road. More than 30,000 people pass through its doors every day to shop in one of 300 departments spread over five floors; its post-Christmas sale attracts 10 times that many people. If your time is limited, don't miss the Art Deco food halls on the ground floor. Open 10:00–18:00, Monday, Tuesday and Saturday; 10:00–19:00, Wednesday–Friday. Nearby **Harvey Nichols** (known as 'Harvey Nicks' to its regular customers) is another top department store much favoured by the Sloane set.

> ### HARRODS
>
> This internationally famous store, which was originally a tea-dealer's shop in the City, moved into Knightsbridge in 1849 and began selling perfumes, medicines and stationery, as well as groceries. By 1880 it employed nearly 100 assistants, and in 1898 installed London's first escalator – with a member of staff standing at the top ready to revive customers with brandy and smelling salts. The present building, which is illuminated at night, dates from 1905. Today, Harrods employs over 3000 staff and is owned by the Egyptian Al Fayed brothers.

PALACE RESIDENTS

The royal residents of Kensington Palace seem to have suffered more than their share of gruesome deaths. William III's wife, Mary, died of smallpox in the palace at the age of 32, having bravely ordered all those not infected to leave the premises. Her sister Anne died of apoplexy, brought on by over-eating, in the blue bedroom. George II also died of apoplexy – in the lavatory. The chubby future Queen Victoria spent a lonely, unhappy childhood in this palace, and when she acceded to the throne at just 18 years of age, she held her first Privy Council meeting in the Red Saloon (also included in the tour).

Opposite above:
Model boating is popular on the Round Pond in Kensington Gardens.
Below: *Kensington Palace houses royal apartments but a part of it is also open to the public.*

KENSINGTON
Kensington Gardens ★★

The westerly extension of Hyde Park, Kensington Gardens were once the private grounds of Kensington Palace. The Gardens became a public park in 1841, and now merge seamlessly with Hyde Park itself. The delightful gardens feature several ornamental fountains and statues – the latter including Jacob Epstein's Rima as well as the famous statue of J M Barrie's fictional Peter Pan by George Frampton (dating from 1912) which has sculpted squirrels, mice, rabbits, birds and fairies cavorting at its base. The Round Pond, just near Kensington Palace, is very popular with children (and indeed adults) piloting model boats. There are plans to create some form of memorial garden to Diana, Princess of Wales, who lived in Kensington Palace until her death in 1997.

Kensington Palace ★★

Kensington Palace, at the western end of Kensington Gardens, was originally a modest country mansion before being transformed by William of Orange in 1689. The Palace currently provides apartments for Prince and Princess Michael of Kent, the Duke and Duchess of Gloucester, and Princess Margaret.

The **State Apartments** have recently re-opened after a £2.5 million facelift; the main highlights are the **trompe l'oeil** galleries above the King's Staircase; the King's Gallery (with works by Rubens and Van Dyck); Queen Victoria's Bedroom, where she woke one morning in June 1837 to find her uncle had died and she was Queen; and the court dress collection. The State Apartments are open daily 10:00–17:00, daily in summer; 10:00–15:00, Wednesday–Sunday in winter. Take tea in the superb **Orangery**, originally built for Queen Anne. Open 09:30 to dusk, daily (Closed Christmas).

AROUND KENSINGTON

Kensington High Street has a range of shops from department stores such as **Barkers** to small boutiques, plus two interesting indoor clothing and accessory markets, **Hype** and **Kensington Market**. Running north from St Mary Abbots church is **Kensington Church Street** which specializes in antiques. You'll find several good French patisseries and bakeries near the **Institut Français** (Queensberry Place) in South Kensington.

The Commonwealth Institute*

The Commonwealth Institute, situated at the western end of Kensington High Street, currently houses a cavernous exhibition on the history, landscapes, wildlife and culture of the 50 Commonwealth countries.

Holland Park **

This charming park covers just 22ha (54 acres) but within it there are woodland areas (at their best in May, when the azaleas and rhododendrons are in bloom), rose gardens, formal flower gardens, an iris garden and a Japanese garden (created for the 1991 London Festival of Japan). The park, open from 7:30 to dusk throughout the year, was once the private garden of 17th-century Holland House, largely destroyed by Nazi bombing in World War II. The remains of the house now contain a youth hostel and restaurant (in the former orangery), whilst the terrace is used as an open-air theatre during summer. In Holland Park Road is **Leighton House**, home of the 19th century artist Lord Leighton. Open 11:00–17:30 Monday–Saturday.

Below: *Holland Park, although not large, includes impressive gardens and blooms.*

Above: *The V and A charts the history of art and design through the ages.*
Opposite: *Modelled on a Roman amphitheatre, the Royal Albert Hall is one the capital's largest concert halls.*

THE GREAT EXHIBITION

The Great Exhibition of 1851 was visited by 6 million people and the profits were used to buy 35ha (86 acres) of land in South Kensington, where Prince Albert's vision of a metropolis for the Science and Arts was created. Besides the museums themselves, other insitutions which were developed included the Royal Geographical Society, the Royal College of Organists, and the headquarters of the Royal College of Art.

SOUTH KENSINGTON

Situated between Knightsbridge and Kensington is South Kensington, an area renowned for its high-Victorian architecture, largely the vision of Queen Victoria's consort, Prince Albert.

Victoria and Albert Museum ★★★

Housing the world's largest collection of decorative art and design pieces, the huge Victoria and Albert Museum requires more than just one visit. Founded with proceeds from the Great Exhibition of 1851, it is known simply as the V and A. Open 10:00–18:00, Tuesday–Sunday; 12:00–18:00, Monday.

Its 145 galleries house an extraordinary range of displays which include the world's most comprehensive jewellery collection, the UK's largest dress collection, major collections of British paintings, sculptures, musical instruments and furniture and the largest exhibition of Indian art outside of India.

Natural History Museum ★★★

The Romanesque-style exterior of the Natural History Museum on Exhibition Road may look forbidding, but the interior houses many interesting interactive exhibits and imaginative displays on the natural world – many geared specifically to children, although they are of course also an important resource for students and zoologists.

On entering the main building you are immediately confronted with a massive, 26m (83ft) skeleton of a *Diplodocus*, signalling one of the museum's major attractions for the younger generation, with their enduring fascination with dinosaurs. This is fully exploited in the superb **Dinosaur Gallery** which features life-size animatronic models dramatically tearing each other apart, including the *Tyrannosaurus rex* and many other species. Another highly popular display is **Creepy Crawlies**, with enlarged models of all sorts of insects and spiders. Open 10:00–18:00, Monday–Saturday; 11:00–18:00, Sunday.

Science Museum **

Another colossus – best digested in manageable chunks – the Science Museum has more than 10,000 exhibits on seven floors, covering everything from early transport to space travel and chemistry to telecommunications. Nearly 2000 of the museum's displays are interactive.

They start on the ground floor with the **History of Power**, featuring some massive old steam engines. The interesting **Space Gallery** starts with the earliest known rockets and progresses through to a full-scale mock-up of the moon-landings programme. On the first floor the popular **Launch Pad** section has numerous hands-on displays for children.

There is much more to explore, but another of the main highlights is the cavernous **Flight Lab**, on the third floor, where the displays are bound to enthrall both young and old alike. Open 10:00–18:00 daily.

Royal Albert Hall and Albert Memorial *

The vast edifice of the Royal Albert Hall was completed in 1871 and since its completion has witnessed everything from rock concerts to religious revival meetings. Its most high-profile performances are now the annual Promenade Concerts. Opposite the Royal Albert Hall, in Kensington Gardens, is the Albert Memorial, completed in 1876. It has a spire inlaid with semi-precious stones and a frieze depicting 169 life-size figures of scientists, poets, painters, musicians and architects.

The memorial has recently been restored, returning it to its original Victorian Gothic splendour, adorned with gilded angels and bright mosaics. The seated figure of Prince Albert. holding a catalogue of the Great Exhibition, has been coated with two layers of gold leaf, as he was originally.

WILDLIFE GARDEN

The Natural History Museum's first 'living exhibition' opened recently in the form of a **Wildlife Garden**, intended as both an outdoor classroom and living laboratory. The acre garden has 950 trees, 3800 shrubs, and 20,000 wildflowers, and is landscaped to recreate natural sites such as oak and bluebell woods, marshes and ponds, and wildflower meadows.

THE PROMENADE CONCERTS

From July to September each year the Royal Albert Hall hosts a series of virtuoso classical performances under the umbrella of the **Henry Wood Promenade Concerts** (usually known as 'the Proms'). The atmosphere is particularly lively on the famous Last Night of the Proms. Apply in writing for tickets, usingBBC Proms Guide, available from bookshops and newsagents.

CHELSEA

A short walk from either Knightsbridge or South Kensington, Chelsea has always been a mecca for dedicated followers of fashion. Chelsea is still one of *the* places to see and be seen, to shop – for everything from cult clubwear to classic brand-name clothes – and to spot famous rock stars, royalty or supermodels. It rose to fame in the 1960s with the arrival of 'Swinging London', when the 'Chelsea set' dictated fashion trends (the miniskirt being one of them) which the world followed. The pattern was repeated again in the late 1970s with the creation of punk. Chelsea still keeps abreast of the times, and many of London's sassiest young designers are based here today.

Running through the heart of Chelsea is **King's Road**, with **Sloane Square** at one end, and World's End at the other, choc-a-bloc with trendy shoe shops, indoor antique markets, fashion boutiques, bars and coffee shops. Although perhaps not as star-studded now as it once was, it is still a fun place to be – particularly on Saturday afternoons, when it is at its busiest. King's Road was initially a farmers' track which passed through Chelsea's market gardens. It later became a private royal thoroughfare used by King Charles II as a way of avoiding carriage congestion when visiting his mistress, Nell Gwynne in Fulham. It was most likely a short cut to Hampton Court.

Chelsea is also famous for its Royal Hospital, the grounds of which house the annual Chelsea Flower Show.

Just across either the beautiful Albert Bridge or Battersea Bridge, on the other side of the Thames, is Battersea, which underwent considerable gentrification in the 1980s. Today, with Battersea Park at its heart, it boasts many little wine bars and smart shops.

Below: *A typical street in Chelsea. One of London's smarter areas, it boasts many elegant townhouses.*

Left: Chelsea Pensioners, in their characteristic scarlet uniforms and medals, are part of the Chelsea landscape.

Chelsea Embankment *

One of the most famous addresses in Chelsea is **Cheyne Walk**, whose Georgian and Queen Anne houses looked right over the Thames until the building of the Embankment in 1874. Among the many celebrities who have lived here are novelists Henry James (No. 21) and George Eliot (No. 4); pre-Raphaelite painter Dante Gabriel Rossetti (No. 16); artists Whistler (No. 93) and Turner (No. 118) and, more recently, pop stars Mick Jagger (No. 48) and Keith Richard (No. 3). Just around the corner at 24 Cheyne Row is **Carlyle's House** where historian Thomas Carlyle's personal effects have been kept as they were when he died in 1881. Open 11:00–17:00, Wednesday–Sunday, April–October.

Chelsea Physic Garden **

One of the great delights of Chelsea is this little-known garden in Royal Hospital Road. It marks the beginning of Cheyne Walk and is the second oldest botanical garden in the country after Oxford's. It was founded by the Society of Apothecaries in 1673 and used to teach physicians the medicinal uses of plants and herbs from all over the world. The Chelsea Physic Garden contains over 5000 plants, including the country's largest outdoor olive tree. At the entrance, maps are available with a list of the most interesting flowers and shrubs. Open 12:00–17:00, Wednesday, 14:00–18:00 Sunday, April–October.

THOMAS MORE

The 16th-century scholar and statesman **Thomas More**, martyred by Henry VIII in 1535, was a long-term resident of Chelsea. He is commemorated by a statue on the Chelsea Embankment, at the end of Cheyne Walk.

CHELSEA SHOPS

King's Road is no longer as fashionable as it was in the 1960s, but there are still lots of top name shops here, as well as some good pubs and restaurants. Signs of the times are a branch of Marks and Spencer and a Safeway supermarket. Further west, towards World's End, are a number of antique shops, including the indoor Chelsea Antiques Market.

6
The City, the East End and Docklands

The City of London, as it is known, is London's commercial and financial heartland. The area, steeped in history, includes many famous sights and institutions, including the Bank of England, the Royal Exchange, the Stock Exchange, the Monument to the Great Fire of London, the Central Criminal Court at the Old Bailey and the Mansion House which is the residence of the Lord Mayor of London.

The most enduring legacy from medieval times is the fascinating **Tower of London**, begun by William the Conqueror and completed in the 14th century. Along with Christopher Wren's masterpiece – **St Paul's Cathedral** – the Tower is not to be missed.

Fuelled by deregulation of financial services in the 1980s, the City underwent a building boom which resulted in developments such as the **Broadgate Centre** and the controversial **Lloyd's of London** building (*see* p. 75).

The East End is traditionally a working class district where the main attractions today are the excellent markets, which are mostly found in the **Whitechapel** and **Spitalfields** districts immediately to the east of the City.

To the east of the City is the area known as **Docklands**, best viewed from a pleasure boat coursing up the Thames. Not the most obvious of tourist attractions within the capital, it is nevertheless a fascinating area – not least because it is the largest urban regeneration project in the world, a status symbolized by the domineering presence of Cesar Pelli's 245m (803ft) high **Canary Wharf Tower**, Britain's tallest building and the second highest in Europe.

DON'T MISS

*** Tower of London: an interesting guided tour, led by Beefeaters, including the **Crown Jewels**.
*** Tower Bridge: views from this walkway as well as the Golden Gallery at the top of **St Paul's Cathedral**.
** Museum of London: charts the fascinating history of London.
** Docklands: ride on the elevated railway, connecting to the **foot tunnel** under the Thames to Greenwich.
* Markets: the bustling East End at weekends.

Opposite: *Night-time illuminations reveal the grand façade of St Paul's.*

Above: *The Royal Exchange. The City is a major centre for international business.*

THE CITY

The City of London, often called the 'Square Mile' because of its compact dimensions, is contained more or less within the area that was originally covered by Roman Londinium. It was almost destroyed in the Great Fire of 1666 and suffered again in the Blitz of 1940, but there is still plenty of interest to see. Although full of modern buildings, the City's streets and alleys still largely follow the Medieval layout.

St Paul's Cathedral ✶✶✶

An unmistakable landmark in the City, St Paul's presents a magnificent façade from the west side, with its two baroque towers capped by a 111m (364ft) dome (second only in size to St Peter's in Rome). Wren's airy design is immediately apparent on entering the main interior (open 08:30–16:00, Monday–Saturday), with the impressive dome featuring a series of trompe l'oeil frescos on the life of St Paul. In the north aisle of the nave is a bronze and marble monument to the Duke of Wellington. In the North Transept is Holman Hunt's famous *The Light of the World*.

The enormous, brightly lit crypt is reached via a flight of stairs in the South Transept, and contains some 350 memorials and over 100 tombs. Recent additions include a memorial to British troops who died in the Falklands, but pride of place goes to the tombs of Wellington and Nelson. Artists (such as Turner and Reynolds) are buried here, as is scientist Alexander Fleming, and Wren himself, whose epitaph reads: *'reader, if you seek his monument, look around you'*.

The first of the three galleries under the dome is the Whispering Gallery; the second is the Stone Gallery, and the third the Golden Gallery (627 steps up) with fabulous views over the City.

Fleet Street *

Once the home of most of Britain's national newspapers, Fleet Street was a popular haunt of scribes and clerks from the 15th century onwards. In 1702 Britain's first daily newspaper, the *Daily Courant*, was published here, and from the 19th century onwards nearly every major paper had printing presses in the vicinity.

Behind the Reuters building you'll find **St Bride's**, known as the 'journalists' church', which was designed by Wren and contains a small museum of Fleet Street history. Open 08:30–17:00, Monday–Saturday. Just off Fleet Street to the north in Gough Square is **Dr Johnson's House**, which was home to the great writer and lexicographer from 1747–59. The house contains some rather unusual memorabilia as well as etchings and portraits of Dr Johnson and his biographer, Boswell. Open 11:00–17:00, Monday–Saturday.

The Barbican Complex *

This large, concrete-clad residential complex was built in the 1970s. At the heart of it is the **Barbican Arts Centre** (a confusing warren covering nine levels, three of them underground), which is home to the Royal Shakespeare Company, the London Symphony Orchestra, the Guildhall School of Music and Drama, cinemas and a concert hall. For details and times of performances, tel: (0171) 638-8891.

YE OLDE CHESHIRE CHEESE

Just off Fleet Street (Wine Office Court, 145 Fleet Street), **Ye Olde Cheshire Cheese** is one of the oldest inns in the City, with parts of the building dating back to 1667. It was popular with the diarist Pepys in the 17th century, and later with Dr Johnson. Charles Dickens and Mark Twain were also, at different times, regular customers. The dark, wood-panelled interior is divided into several snug bars (as was the custom in old inns), with real fires blazing in each.

Below: *The ceiling of St Paul's Cathedral, by Wren, is one of London's most familiar sights and merits a leisurely visit.*

THE GREAT FIRE

The **Great Fire** of 1666 was sparked off by an unattended baker's oven in Pudding Lane on 2 September. Winds quickly fanned the flames but the Lord Mayor, awakened to the news, dismissed the danger ('a woman might piss it out', he said) before going back to sleep. By mid-morning people were fleeing in droves, and the conflagration was threatening to consume the City. Teams of firefighters pulled down houses to create fire breaks, and managed to save the Tower of London by blowing up the surrounding houses. When the fire had spent its course, four-fifths of London had been destroyed, along with over 13,000 homes and 87 churches; St Paul's, Guildhall and other important buildings were gutted. Incredibly, only nine people died – and the Great Fire had an unexpected side-effect, purging the city of the dreaded plague.

Museum of London ★★

Adjacent to the Barbican Complex, the Museum of London features 12 main galleries charting the history of the capital from prehistoric times up until World War II. The museum also presents lectures, films and special events.

The museum displays the history of London from prehistoric times, and offers a most impressive account of the Roman era in its **Roman London Gallery**, where over 2000 original objects, including the latest archaeological finds from around the city, show how its Roman inhabitants would have lived.

There are recreations of a Roman street, public baths, a forum, and the interiors of citizens' houses, as well as wonderful mosaics, sculptures, and a fascinating model of the old Roman port.

On the same floor the tale continues in a chronological order through medieval times to the time of the Great Fire of London in 1666. Highlights of these sections include the **Cheapside Hoard** (a spectacular display of jewellery dating from the mid-16th century) and the **Great Fire Experience** (a small diorama with a tape recounting diarist Samuel Pepys's dramatic first-hand account of the fire).

Downstairs the display begins with the Stuart period, continuing to the 18th century, a time of growth for the city as a major mercantile centre. Other sections include recreated Victorian streets, an Art Deco lift from Selfridges, and the gilded red and gold Lord Mayor's Coach. Open 10:00–17:50, Tuesday–Saturday; 12:00–17:50, Sunday.

Guildhall ★

In the heart of the City, the Guildhall has been London's administrative centre for over 800 years and still houses the offices of the Corporation of London. The Great Hall (open 10:00–17:00, weekdays) features coats of arms and banners from the City's guilds and livery companies. A new art gallery has been built next door to house the Guildhall's extensive art collection and is due to open in 1999.

Lloyd's of London *

Lloyd's of London started out as a society of underwriters who met in a City coffee house (after which the company took its name), and is now one of the world's biggest insurance underwriters. This avant-garde steel and glass building, designed by Richard Rogers, caused something of a stir when it was first unveiled in 1986 but, a decade on, Lloyd's is locked in a legal dispute with the architects since much of the building is now corroding away – it may well be shrouded in scaffolding for years to come.

The Tower of London ***

One of the capital's most popular attractions, the Tower of London is an extraordinarily well-preserved medieval fortress which in its heyday housed around 1500 people. Over the last 900 years it has been a royal palace, a prison, an execution site, an armoury, and is today a repository for the Crown Jewels. Open 09:00–17:00 Monday–Saturday, 10:00–17:00 Sunday in summer; 09:00–16:00, Tuesday–Saturday, 10:00–16:00, Sunday and Monday in winter.

DICK WHITTINGTON

The pantomime character of Dick Whittington, with his knapsack and cat, was based on the life of Richard Whittington, a wealthy merchant who first became Mayor of London in 1397. He was a great public benefactor and when he died, childless, in 1423, his fortune was bequeathed to civic works. By the 1500s his rags-to-riches story had become a legend, with Whittington (and his cat) poised to leave the city when he hears the Bow bells ring out 'turn again, Whittington, thrice Lord Mayor of London'. In fact, he was Mayor four times: a stone on Highgate Hill commemorates the spot where he is supposed to have heard the bells. There is also a stained glass window in his honour in St Michael Paternoster Royal in Skinner's Lane in the City.

Opposite: *Lloyd's of London is an architectural landmark in the heart of the City.*
Left: *The Tower of London was used to house prisoners from medieval times.*

BEEFEATERS AND RAVENS

The Tower of London was the city's first zoo, with leopards, elephants, birds and polar bears on display in medieval times. In the 19th century this menagerie was transferred to London Zoo, but the ravens – feeding on scraps from the palace kitchens and, it is said, pecking away at severed heads from executions – stayed on. An old legend has it that 'only so long as they stay will the White Tower stand' and since Charles II's time they have been protected by royal decree.

The centre of the complex is the **White Tower**, which dates back to the time of William the Conqueror. Inside are displays of arms and armour, including some used by Henry VIII. There is also an exhibition of torture instruments along with an axe and block used for executions at the Tower. On the first floor is the beautiful 11th century **St. John's Chapel**, the oldest church in London.

In the northeastern corner is the **Martin Tower**, which houses a new exhibition, Crowns and Diamonds, which includes some rare 18th and 19th century crown frames used at coronations.

Many prisoners arrived at the Tower by boat, entering via the **Traitor's Gate** before being incarcerated in one of the many fortified towers surrounding Tower Green, in the middle of the complex. Directly behind the Traitor's Gate is the **Bloody Tower**, where the 12-year-old Edward V and his 10-year-old brother, the Duke of York, were murdered on the orders of Richard III. On the west side of the Bloody Tower is the **Queen's House** (now the home of the Tower's Governor and closed to the public) which was built by Henry VIII and used as a prison for Katherine Howard, Anne Boleyn and Lady Jane Grey; the last inmate was Hitler's Deputy, Rudolph Hess.

Nearby is **Tower Green**, the site of several executions, and the spot is marked by a plaque listing the

Above: *Beefeaters have been guarding the Tower since Henry VIII's time.*
Right: *The Queen's House in the Tower of London.*
Opposite: *The road across Tower Bridge is still raised periodically to allow ships to pass underneath.*

names of the victims. These
include two of Henry VIII's
wives, Anne Boleyn and
Katharine Howard, Lady Jane
Grey, the nine day queen, and
the Earl of Essex, Elizabeth I's
favourite. Behind is the church
of **St Peter ad Vincula**, where
they were all buried, without
any memorial.

On the northern side of the
compound the **Crown Jewels**
are on display in the Waterloo
Barracks. A moving walkway
system carries you past them
at a fairly fast pace. The
sparkling exhibits include the
Crown of State (bedecked with thousands of jewels
including a 317-carat diamond), the Koh-i-Noor diamond, sceptres, orbs and other glittering regal
paraphernalia.

Tower Bridge ★★

Tower Bridge is a marvel of Victorian engineering (it took
eight years to build) and was first opened to traffic on 30
June 1894. It was designed so that tall sailing ships could
reach the Port of London – ships still have precedence
over road traffic, although compared to the early years
(when it was raised over 6000 times a year) it is now
raised only about 500 times a year. The 1,000 ton bascules
were originally raised using pure hydraulic power, but
electricity is used today.

The bridge was built in the Gothic style to blend in
with the Tower of London, but beneath its stonework
exterior is a massive steel frame which you can see when
you get inside. Guided tours lead through a series of
videos and displays (including an animatronic Cockney
bridge painter) on the bridge's history. Views from the
top walkways are terrific. Open 10:00–18:30 daily in summer; 09:30–18:00 in winter.

CEREMONIES AT THE TOWER

The Changing of the Guard
takes place daily at 13:00 on
Tower Green. The 700-year-
old traditional **Ceremony of
the Keys** takes place nightly
at 21:53, as the Chief
Yeoman Warder locks the
Tower gates and performs a
ritual exchange which has
remained unchanged since
Queen Elizabeth I's reign. For
tickets to witness this ancient
ceremony, write two months
in advance to HM Tower of
London, London EC3N 4AB,
enclose an SAE and names
and addresses of all group
members. **Royal Gun Salutes**
mark royal birthdays and
other state occasions. The
Beating of the Bounds,
which takes place every three
years on Ascension Day, is
also medieval in origin (the
idea was to define the parish
boundaries).

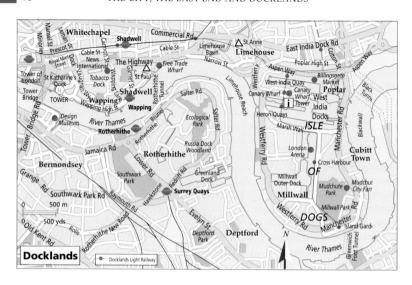

Docklands

◆━ Docklands Light Railway

THE EAST END AND DOCKLANDS

The East End has a colourful past and has been a focal point for immigrants and refugees, from the Huguenots through to Irish, Jews, and Bengalis. Recently, the East End has acquired a new lease of life as a focus for contemporary art, with hundreds of artists living and working in the area (including the *enfant terrible* of the contemporary art world, Damien Hirst). Several influential galleries are located here, including the famed Whitechapel Art Gallery.

Street Markets ★

Of all the markets in this area, one of the best-known is in **Petticoat Lane** (mostly clothing), which has existed for over 200 years. Just to the north is the **Spitalfields market**, once the centre of the fruit and vegetable trade (now mostly crafts and food). East of here and at the heart of London's Bengali community, **Brick Lane** market (bric-a-brac and clothes) tempts passers-by with the aroma of curry wafting out from behind the stalls. **Columbia Road** is an enjoyable street filled with plant and flower stalls. All these markets are best on the weekends. The nearest tube stations are Liverpool Street and Aldgate East.

DECLINE OF THE DOCKS

Most of the dock system was built from the 19th century onwards, with the biggest docks being the vast Royal Docks, each 1.6km (5½ miles) long, with massive warehouses protected behind high walls to keep out thiefs. The development of containerized shipping (for which a new port was built at Tilbury in the 1960s) and other factors eventually led to all the docks being shut down between 1968 and 1981. The area became an urban wasteland until regeneration began in the 1980s, when the London Docklands Development Corporation (LDDC) was set up, and developers moved into the new Enterprise Zone. Today, there are over 2000 businesses in the area employing some 70,000 people.

Whitechapel Art Gallery ★

One of London's top contemporary art galleries is in the heart of the East End: the Whitechapel Art Gallery was founded by a Victorian philanthropist and today often stages unusual exhibitions of avant-garde art from around the world. Open 11:00–17:00, Tuesday–Sunday, 11:00–20:00, Wednesday.

Bethnal Green Museum of Childhood★

The museum houses a superb collection of toys and games past and present, including teddy bears, doll's houses and puppets. Open 10:00–17:50, Monday–Thursday and Saturday; 14:30–17:40, Sunday.

Docklands ★

Best known for its hotch-potch of architectural styles, Docklands offers charming riverside pubs, restored warehouses, sailing ships, and even an urban farm where you can go horse riding. Docklands is a catch-all term for a vast area extending east from London Bridge along the Thames, covering 22km² (8½ sq miles), bigger than the City of London and West End combined, with over 88km (55 miles) of waterfront. The most accessible area is **St Katherine's Dock**, east of the Tower, where there is a marina, old swing bridges and a famous 18th-century pub, the **Dickens' Inn**. Take the canal walk to **Tobacco Dock**; a pair of old sailing ships are moored nearby. Further east, **Limehouse,** home to the city's first Chinese community, once linked the docks with the canal network. Hawksmoor's St Anne's Church, distinguished by its church clock, which is the highest in the City. The **Isle of Dogs** is now the commercial and business hub of Docklands, and **West India Docks** is home to the massive **Canary Wharf** development. Beyond are the **Royal Docks** and London City Airport.

> **VISITING DOCKLANDS**
>
> One of the best ways to see the new developments in Docklands is to take a boat trip from Westminster, Charing Cross or Tower piers to Greenwich. To get into the heart of Docklands take the Docklands Light Railway (DLR) from Bank or Tower Gateway station. The DLR is a fully-automated, elevated rail system carrying some 60,000 people every day. If you travel all the way to Island Gardens you can walk through a tunnel under the Thames to Greenwich. You will soon be able to reach Greenwich direct by DLR, via a new tunnel being built under the Thames.

Below: *St Katherine's Dock was one of the first of the old docks to undergo redevelopment.*

7
North London

The dividing line between Central and North London follows the busy traffic route of Marylebone and Euston Roads. Once known as New Road, this was the city's first by-pass, built in 1756 to allow cattle to be herded from west of the city to Smithfield market without clogging up Oxford Street. The main attraction on Marylebone Road is **Madame Tussaud's** waxworks museum, one of London's most popular sights; you can combine a visit to Madame Tussaud's with the **Planetarium** next door to it.

North of Marylebone road is **Regent's Park**, laid out in the early 1800s and home to **London Zoo** since 1834. Winding its way around the park's northern edge and passing through the zoo itself is the **Regent's Canal**, built to link the Grand Junction Canal at Paddington (which led in turn to the thriving industrial north) with the docks.

Beyond Regent's Park is elegant **Hampstead**, whose village-like atmosphere has appealed to artists, writers and celebrities of all kinds for many years. Spreading in a great swathe northwards from Hampstead is **Hampstead Heath**, one of the largest open spaces in the capital encompassing a range of landscapes including untamed woodland, ponds and lakes, meadows and fields. It is a popular venue for all sorts of activities, including open-air concerts at the historic **Kenwood House**.

To the east of Hampstead lies **Camden Town**, one of the capital's favourite weekend venues, with a vast network of market stalls sprawling around the Regent's Canal at Camden Lock. Both **Islington** and **Clerkenwell**, further east, have many unusual attractions.

DON'T MISS

*** **Regent's Park:** a walk along the canalside combined with a visit to **London Zoo**.
*** **Hampstead:** explore the village and the wild spaces of **Hampstead Heath**.
** **Pub theatres:** experience one of Islington's pub theatres and then browse through the antique stalls and shops of **Camden Passage**.
** **Camden:** catch up on the latest fashions in the busy weekend markets here.
* **Madame Tussaud's:** incredible waxworks display.

Opposite: *One of London's many famous graveyards, Highgate Cemetery features an array of unusual statuary.*

Above: *Queen Elizabeth I, one of hundreds of wax dummies at the renowned Madame Tussaud's.*
Below: *Madame Tussaud's and the Planetarium are among London's most popular attractions, so expect long queues!*

MARYLEBONE
Madame Tussaud's ★★

The third most popular tourist attraction in the capital (after the British Museum and National Gallery), this famous waxworks museum attracts over 2.5 million visitors annually, and you should expect to queue to get in (as long as an hour in peak season). Madame Tussaud's waxworks first came to London in 1802, after its eponymous creator was forced to flee the French Revolution, only narrowly escaping the guillotine herself by moulding death masks of the Revolution's victims. Madame Tussaud died in 1850 at the age of 89, and her last work, a self-portrait, is on display in the museum today. Open 10:00–17:30, Monday–Friday; 09:30–17:30, Saturday and Sunday.

The theme settings for the more than 300 waxwork figures within the complex start off with a **Garden Party**, where contemporary celebrities (such as Dudley Moore, Arnold Schwarzenegger and Dame Edna Everage) socialize in a replica of the grounds of an English country house. The **200 Years** display traces the history of modelling techniques from Madame Tussaud's first death mask of Marie Antoinette, through to the latest animatronic figures. **Legends** features stars of stage and screen, and leads through to the **Grand Hall**, where effigies of the Royal Family and world military leaders and statesmen stand proudly in full regalia.

The most popular section is undoubtedly the **Chamber of Horrors**, which was completely remodelled in 1996 to make it even more spine-chilling than before. Torture, dismemberment, mass murderers, Dracula, and Jack the Ripper are all on the menu here – although many of these scenarios are better presented in the London Dungeon (*see* p. 99). Finally, there is the **Spirit of London**, a journey

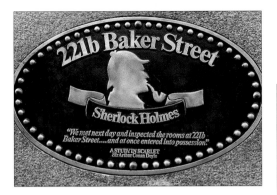

Left: *A plaque marks the site of Sherlock Holmes' house in Baker Street.*

LONDON CENTRAL MOSQUE

On the western edge of Regent's Park, the **London Central Mosque** is testament to the continuing religious and architectural diversity of the capital. Completed in 1978, it features a shining copper dome and minaret with a hall of worship beneath which is capable of holding up to 1800 people. The interior is decorated along traditional Islamic lines. Visitors are welcome at the information centre (shoes must be removed, and women must use a separate gallery).

through the history of the capital in miniaturized black taxi cabs. The tour starts in the court of Elizabeth I in the 16th century, continues through to the **Great Fire of London**, and progresses through the Industrial Revolution, the Blitz during the World War II, to the Swinging London of the 60s.

Planetarium **

The Planetarium, next door to Madame Tussaud's, is equally popular. Other than the main star shows, the Planetarium features a **Space Trail** with models of planets, satellites and spacecraft, plus interactive touch-screen computers, and live weather pictures. The main auditorium features a 30-minute **Star Show**, using images from spacecraft and satellites woven together with a narrative on space travel, planets and the stars. Open 11:30–17:00, Monday–Friday; 09:30–17:00, Saturday and Sunday.

Sherlock Holmes Museum *

Sir Arthur Conan Doyle's fictional Victorian detective, Sherlock Holmes, had his home at 221b Baker Street. The Sherlock Holmes Museum is a faithful reconstruction of his house as it might have been. It is, in fact, located at 236 Baker Street, even though the sign on the door says otherwise. Open 09:30–18:00. The theme is continued in the tea room, Hudson's Restaurant, which is on the ground floor.

REGENT'S CANAL

Running in a meandering path through north and east London down to the Thames at Limehouse, **Regent's Canal** was completed in 1820 and is still in use by narrowboats today. One of the most attractive sections is the small basin known as **Little Venice**, in Maida Vale (tube: Warwick Avenue) from where you can catch a **waterbus** down to **London Zoo** (which has its own jetty) and then on down to **Camden Lock**. The service runs hourly from 10:00-17:00 in summer (details from the London Waterbus Company, tel: (0171) 482-2550).

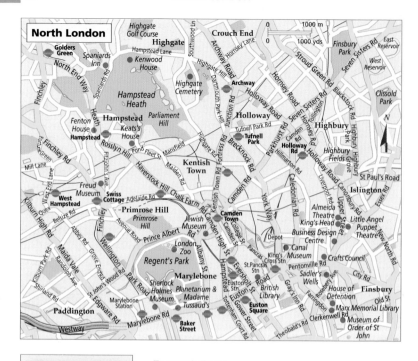

North London

Smart residential **St John's Wood** is home to England's most famous cricket venue, **Lord's Cricket Ground**, which is owned by the Marylebone Cricket Club (MCC). Tours of the ground and museum are available most days at 12:00 and 14:00; Tel: (0171) 432-1033 for details. Between tube station and cricket ground is **Abbey Road Studios** where the **Beatles** recorded much of their work during the 1960s. Paul McCartney still has a house nearby. For guided tours of Beatles' London: Original London Walks, tel: (0171) 624-3978.

REGENT'S PARK

Extending north from Marylebone Road up towards Hampstead and Camden, Regent's Park is best known as the home of London Zoo, and the elegant Regency terraces (designed by John Nash) which surround it. It was once a thickly wooded area (and the private hunting grounds of Henry VIII) until Cromwell felled most of its 1600 trees to help build ships for the Navy.

Nash and the Prince Regent (later George IV) envisaged a belt of grand terraced houses around the outside of the park, and although the scheme was never completed, Nash's legacy is still visible in the cream-coloured stucco of **Chester Terrace** and **Cumberland Terrace**, and the architecturally diverse houses of **Park Village West**. The **Open-Air Theatre** in the Inner Circle was popular in the 1930s for its productions of *A Midsummer Night's Dream*, and Shakespeare's plays are still staged here on warm summer evenings. The nearby **Queen Mary's Gardens** have one of the country's best rose displays. Beyond Prince Albert Row is **Primrose Hill**, well worth the climb to enjoy sweeping panoramas of the city.

London Zoo ★★

Covering 14ha (34½ acres) of the northern corner of Regent's Park, the London Zoo has endured its fair share of ups and downs – including the recent threat of complete closure due to a funding crisis – since it was first opened by the Zoological Society of London in 1828.

London Zoo is one of the world's oldest (and on a restricted site), and so cannot be compared with more modern zoos elsewhere in the world. It has, however, long been at the forefront of zoological studies and scientific research into animal genetics, ecology, behaviour, and reproduction, and can claim many firsts, including the public aquarium (1849), the reptile house (1853), the insect house (1881), and a children's zoo (1938).

The zoo also contains nine listed buildings, including Mappin Terraces (intended to resemble a mountain landscape for bears and other animals), the much-loved penguin pool, giraffe house and Snowdon Aviary.

But of course it is the animals that people come to see, and with 12,000 of them here there is plenty to observe and enjoy, from the tiniest tree snails in the invertebrate house to the Asian jumbos in the elephant house. Kids can feed and handle animals in the **Ambika Paul Children's Zoo**, watch the elephants being weighed, peer at possums and other creatures of the night in Moonlight World, ride on a camel, or watch parrots, owls, lemurs, and cats show off their special skills in the Animals in Action presentation. Open 10:00–17:30, daily in summer; 10:00–16:00 in winter.

THE FUTURE ZOO

As part of its 'Zoo 2005' project, London Zoo is focusing more on endangered animals (97 species present here are facing extinction in the wild) and building a vast new glass-fronted pavilion dedicated to conservation education. Other projects in the pipeline include a centre for the conservation of Madagascar species, a new hi-tech World of Invertebrates, and a revamped Aquarium. The Mappin Terraces are to be re-opened as an enormous gorilla enclosure.

Below: *The Snowdon Aviary rises up majestically alongside Regent's Canal at London Zoo.*

Camden has a proliferation
of good pubs, many of
them with live music and
most packed to overflowing
at weekends. Some of the
more popular ones include
the **Oxford Arms** (a traditional pub with an outdoor
beer garden and good bar
food), the **Engine Room**
(a funky little pub, also with
good bar food), the **Hawley
Arms** (one of the oldest 'in'
places with locals and bikers),
the **Fusilier and Firkin**
(excellent locally-brewed
beers, good food, live music)
and the **Man-in-the-Moon**
(relaxed atmosphere, real
ales, good value for food).

CAMDEN TOWN

Another of London's more Bohemian 'village suburbs',
Camden Town is popular among Londoners for its
extensive **markets**, of which there are several at either
side of **Camden Lock** on the Regent's Canal. You may
well find designer clothes here before they become
household names. At weekends it buzzes with activity
and scores of shops, trendy pubs, bistros and restaurants complement the markets, each with their own
character and style.

The original **Camden Market** has around 120 stalls
where the emphasis is mostly on fashion, jewellery, and
great second-hand clothing, records and tapes. Open
09:00–17:00, Thursday–Sunday. Between this market and
Camden Town tube is the indoor **Electric Ballroom**,
which operates as a market on Sundays only, and which
features up-and-coming fashion and jewellery designers.
Opposite here the **Inverness Street Market** is the oldest
section, and sells fruit and veget-
ables. Open Monday–Saturday.

On the other side of the canal
bridge the **Camden Lock Market**
(open daily) is the main arts and
crafts area, with the many small
boutiques and craft workshops
supplemented at weekends by
hundreds of stalls selling bric-
a-brac, candles, prints, books,
clothes, period clothing and much
more besides.

Between Camden Town tube
and Chalk Farm tube, **Camden
High Street** and **Chalk Farm
Road** (its extension) is the main
drag, lined with interesting stores,
from an alternative bookshop to
cheese and confectionery special-
ists, art galleries, many trendy
shoe shops, and Asian and North
American craft shops.

Left: *Camden Lock market is a popular weekend market, selling clothes, bric-a-brac, books, antiques and collectables.*

Opposite: *St Pancras Station, one of London's most exuberant Victorian buildings.*

On Chalk Farm Road is the **Stables Antique Market** which is the biggest of all the markets, and has some of the best bargains in collectables and antiques, ornaments, furniture, and good quality second-hand clothes. It is open throughout the day on Saturdays and Sundays and is usually quite crowded.

Within a few minutes' walk of Camden Town tube is the **Jewish Museum** at 129 Albert Street, which has a series of stylish galleries on Jewish history in Britain and religious life, and a renowned ceremonial art collection; there are also interesting audio-visual displays explaining the Jewish faith and customs. It includes treasures from London's Great Synagogue which was burnt down during the Second World War. Open 10:00–16:00, Sunday–Thursday; closed on Bank and Jewish holidays.

To the south of Camden Town the area around **King's Cross** railway station is a notorious red-light district, but is soon to be redeveloped as a terminal for the Channel tunnel trains. Alongside King's Cross the old **St Pancras** station, with its magnificent mock-Gothic spires, is a marvel of Victorian architecture, with the much-criticized modern **British Library** looming up alongside it.

Behind King's Cross, canal boats moor up in the King's Cross Basin, where the interesting little **London Canal Museum** traces the social and commercial history of canal boats and the people who have lived and worked on them. Open 10:00–16:30, Tuesday–Sunday.

THE BRITISH LIBRARY

After many delays, technical problems and overspending, the new British Library finally opened on Euston Road in 1997. It houses 12-million books, has 11 specialist reading rooms and three exhibition spaces for the general visitor. Here are displayed such national treasures as two of the surviving four copies of *Magna Carta*, the First Folio of Shakespeare's works, the beautiful 7th-century *Lindisfarne Gospels*, the original manuscript of Lewis Caroll's *Alice in Wonderland* and the score of Handel's *Messiah*.

Above: *The elegant, white-washed façade of Keats's former home in Hampstead.*

HAMPSTEAD

Hampstead was first recorded in the Domesday Book as 'Hampstede', meaning homestead, and consisted of nothing more than a small rural farm. By the 18th century it had become a fashionable spa, selling water to city-dwellers in the aptly-named **Flask Walk**, and later became (as it still is) a popular residence for the wealthy, the intelligentsia and literary set.

Hampstead's steeply sloping village **High Street** features numerous fashion shops, art and antiques galleries, boutiques and craft shops, as well as arty cafés and lively pubs. Surrounding it is a maze of cobblestone lanes, alleyways, elegant houses and Georgian squares.

Hampstead Museums *

Before heading off to the wide open spaces of Hampstead Heath, there are several noteworthy museums in the vicinity. The **Freud Museum,** 20 Maresfield Gardens, (open 12:00–17:00, Wednesday–Sunday) is where Freud lived after escaping from the Nazis in 1938, until his death the following year. His library and study (including the famous couch) have been preserved and the house contains his collection of erotic antiquities and archives.

Another famous Hampstead resident, poet John Keats, is commemorated in **Keats's House** in Wentworth Place where he lived between 1818–20. The Regency villa contains a collection of his books, manuscripts and letters. Open 10:00–13:00 and 14:00–18:00 April–November; 13:00–17:00 December–March weekdays; 10:00–13:00 and 14:00–17:00 Saturdays all year; 14:00–17:00, Sundays all year and Bank Holidays.

Music aficionados shouldn't miss the excellent collection of old musical instruments at **Fenton House** which includes a 1612 harpsichord (played by Handel), and many other unusual old pieces. Open 14:00–17:00, Wednesday–Friday in summer; 11:00–17:00 weekends.

SPANIARDS INN

To the west of Kenwood House at the northern end of Spaniards Road, traffic is forced to slow down as it negotiates a narrow passage between an old toll booth and the historic **Spaniards Inn**, an 18th-century coaching inn. The famous highwayman Dick Turpin is said to have used it as a hiding place and to spy out likely-looking coaches to rob as they left London on the road north. Legend has it that he would fire his pistol nightly as a signal at closing time.

Hampstead Heath **

Hampstead's main attraction is the 300ha (741 acre) expanse of the Heath, one of the most popular parks in London, with woodlands, open fields, heathland, and 28 natural ponds (some are used for swimming or fishing). For great views of Hampstead and the City head for **Parliament Hill**, which is a popular spot for kite-flying. On the northern fringes of the Heath is **Kenwood House**, a

17th-century mansion (remodelled by Robert Adam) which now houses the Iveagh Bequest, a fabulous art collection featuring such famous works as a self-portrait by Rembrandt, Vermeer's *Guitar Player* as well as paintings by Gainsborough and Reynolds. The interior of Kenwood House (particularly Adam's library) is also noteworthy. Open daily 10:00–18:00 in summer; 10:00–16:00 in winter.

Above: *Hampstead Heath is one of the largest and most pleasant of London's parks.*

HIGHGATE

While not as prestigious as neighbouring Hampstead, Highgate has still had its share of famous residents (including Sir Francis Bacon and Samuel Coleridge), and can at least boast one of London's most famous graves, that of **Karl Marx**. Highgate (named after the country's oldest tollgate which once stood in the present-day High Street) has several busy traffic arteries running through it, but it is to visit the extraordinary **Cemetery**, with its mausoleums, catacombs, and bizarre statuary, that most people come here. Others buried here include Christina Rossetti, Charles Dickens's wife Catherine, and author Mary Ann Evans (who wrote as George Eliot).

The **West Cemetery** is the most interesting part, containing as it does numerous impressive vaults and statuary. Open 10:00–17:00 Monday–Friday, 11:00–17:00 Saturday and Sunday in summer; 10:00–16:00 Monday–Friday, 11:00–16:00 Saturday and Sunday in winter.

FAMOUS RESIDENTS

Almost every street in Hampstead seems to have blue plaques commemorating famous residents of the past: William Blake, Agatha Christie, Richard Burton, George Orwell, Robert Louis Stevenson, Charles de Gaulle, John Constable, John le Carré, Henry Moore, Peter Sellers, Barbara Hepworth, A A Milne, and Edith Sitwell are just some of them. More recently, it has been home to celebrities such as Elizabeth Taylor, Sting, Boy George, Tom Conti, Emma Thompson, and Jeremy Irons, to name but a few. Hampstead's standing amongst the literati is well illustrated by the fact that the current local Labour MP is actress Glenda Jackson.

Right: *Colourful barges at Islington Lock on the Regent's Canal. The canal is a pleasant, alternative way to travel through parts of North London.*

ISLINGTON

Like Hampstead, Islington was once a spa resort surrounded by fields but, whereas Hampstead grew in stature, Islington developed into a working class district – a process which has only been partially reversed by an influx of writers, media folk and left-leaning trendies since the 1970s. Today, its main thoroughfare, **Upper Street**, is a lively mix of fashionable bistros, ethnic restaurants, quirky shops and alternative theatre venues, with many attractive Georgian squares tucked away on either side of it.

Opposite Islington Green, the **Business Design Centre's** modern façade hides the venerable Victorian brickwork of the old Royal Agricultural Hall (the 'Aggie'), which was one of the first exhibition halls in the capital. The BDC now hosts trade, antique and art fairs throughout the year. Continuing along Upper Street you reach the **Town Hall** and the **Islington Museum Gallery**, which features a small permanent collection plus temporary exhibitions of local and historical interest. Open 11:00–17:00, Wednesday–Saturday; 14:00–16:00, Sunday, tel: (0171) 354-9442 for details.

At the end of Upper Street the busy Highbury Corner roundabout leads to **Highbury Fields**, one of the few parks in the borough.

Just a short distance from Angel tube on Pentonville Road is the headquarters of the **Crafts Council** housed in a beautifully refurbished 19th-century chapel with

ISLINGTON INFORMATION

Islington's Visitor Information Centre is the first in the country to provide details on local theatres, galleries, and other attractions on the World Wide Web, and computer-literate visitors can access this new service at www.real-london.com. Otherwise, pick up an old-fashioned telephone to find out what's on at the Almeida Theatre, tel: (0171) 359-4404; the King's Head Theatre Club, tel: (0171) 226-1916; the Little Angel Puppet Theatre, tel: (0171) 226-1787; Old Red Lion Theatre, tel: (0171) 837-7816. Pick up the 'Angel Trail', leaflet guiding one on foot through Islington and Clerkenwell, available free from the Discover Islington Info Centre 44 Duncan Street, N1 8BW, tel: (0171) 278-8787.

exhibitions of contemporary crafts which are held throughout the year. Open 11:00–18:00, Tuesday–Saturday; 14:00–18:00, Sunday.

The **Regent's Canal** emerges from a long tunnel connecting it to the King's Cross Basin at the bottom of Duncan Street to the east of Upper Street, and there is a pleasant walk along here with several interesting pubs; you can walk (or cycle) all the way to Limehouse and Docklands.

Camden Passage **

Islington's main attraction is the **antique market** in the pedestrianized precinct of Camden Passage, just a few minutes' walk from the Angel tube; the market itself fills the pedestrian passageway on Wednesdays and Saturdays, but the surrounding antique shops are open all week. The more mundane **Chapel Market** (open daily except Mondays) on the other side of Upper Street is a typically traditional London street market, selling everything from cheap china to food and clothing.

Islington Theatres *

Islington has a lively theatre scene, with several pub theatres (including the famous **King's Head**, where prices are still calculated in pre-decimal pounds, shillings, and pence) and the city's only permanent marionette theatre, the **Little Angel Puppet Theatre**. There is also the **Almeida Theatre** (one of London's premier showcases for new dramatic talent).

Left: *The Old Red Lion Theatre, a popular pub theatre in Islington.*

Right: *St John's Gate, which dates back to the 16th-century, is one of the three medieval establishments that survive today.*

CLERKENWELL

Sandwiched between Holborn and Islington, Clerkenwell is well off the beaten track. It has a long association with craft industries (such as jewellery, cutlers and printing) and its old warehouses house many artisans' workshops. Many of the run-down areas in the district are currently undergoing redevelopment as part of the Corporation of London's plans to revitalize fringe areas around the City.

The jewellery trade is most evident in the opulent displays of **Hatton Garden** (off Holborn Circus) which is still the UK's main centre for trade in gemstones, gold and silver. Clerkenwell also has a long association with radical politics – partly due to the many small printing presses in the vicinity – and Lenin worked here for a while, in a building which now houses the **Marx Memorial Library** on Clerkenwell Green. Open 13:00–18:00 Monday–Thursday, 10:00–13:00 Saturday.

House of Detention ★★

Just north of Clerkenwell Green is another new 'prison museum' to add to the growing list of horror-style attractions in the capital. Built on one of London's earliest prison sites – dating back to 1616 – the House of Detention has recently been excavated to reveal the dank, spooky underground chambers where prisoners were incarcerated. A 15-minute guided tour is accompanied by suitably dramatic audio-visual effects. Open daily 10:00–18:00.

LITTLE ITALY

During the second half of the 19th century Italian immigrants were much in demand for their skills as painters, artisans (who created fine plasterwork ceilings) and even as dancing and fencing teachers. The Italian community established its own **Little Italy** in Clerkenwell around Rosebery Avenue, Farringdon Road and Clerkenwell Road. Its main focal point was **St Peter's Italian Church** and although nowadays the 10,000 Italians who originally crowded into this area have settled elsewhere, where there are still Italian restaurants, delicatessens and wine merchants in the vicinity.

Museum of the Order of St John ✶

In the 13th century, Clerkenwell was the base of the cru-
sading Knights Hospitallers (their rivals, the Knights
Templar, had their base in the Temple), and the remains
of their priory of the Order of St John at Jerusalem are
found to the southeast of Clerkenwell Green. The most
conspicuous remnant is **St John's Gate**, which now forms
part of the museum, and which charts the development of
the Order and contains a comprehensive collection of historical items. Guided tours (11:00 and 14:30, Tuesday,
Friday and Saturday) include visits to the rooms inside
the Gatehouse and Chapter Hall, as well as the ancient
crypt in the Grand Priory Church. Open 10:00–17:00,
Monday–Friday; 10:00–16:00, Saturday.

> **MOUNT PLEASANT**
>
> Post offices don't normally
> feature much as tourist
> attractions but the
> **Mount Pleasant Sorting
> Office** – the largest in the
> country – is unique in that
> it has its own private under-
> ground railway system which
> shuttles down a network
> of tunnels to other sorting
> offices, a miniature
> (and driverless) version
> of the tube. Viewing is
> by arrangement (write to
> the Post office Controller,
> 148–164 Old Street, EC1).

Charterhouse ✶

A few minutes' walk from St John's Gate, Charterhouse
was a Carthusian monastery from the 14th to the 17th
centuries, and was later converted into a private charity
school. The school itself moved to Surrey in the mid 19th
century. The complex of buildings includes several of the
original **monks' cells** as well as the **Masters' Court**, with
Renaissance ornamentation in its superb **Great Hall** and
Great Chamber. Charterhouse can only be visited on
guided tours at 14:15 on Wednesdays, April–July.

Below: *Rebuilt during
Tudor times, Charter-
house was originally a
Carthusian monastery.*

8
South and
Southeast London

A lmost all London's major institutions are north of the Thames, so it is easy to dismiss the area to the south as merely residential, with little of interest to offer visitors. But this is far from the truth, as long-standing institutions such as the **South Bank Centre**, and a host of interesting new developments, add immeasurably to the city's cultural heritage.

The South Bank Centre, which is Europe's largest arts complex, is about to undergo a facelift (*see* p. 97). Nearby the massive Bankside Power Station (which closed in 1980) is being developed by the Tate Gallery into a spectacular new museum of modern art. Film and television buffs will enjoy a visit to the **Museum of the Moving Image** (MOMI). Further east, in Southwark, the inspirational **Globe Theatre** has recently opened its doors to stage plays as they were performed in Shakespeare's day. Southwark is also home to **Southwark Cathedral**, which was built in the 13th and 14th centuries. There are also a number of historic pubs and inns to visit.

On the other side of London Bridge station a cluster of tourist attractions (such as **Britain at War** and the **London Dungeon**) are attracting people across Tower Bridge, and the **Design Museum** is at the heart of the rejuvenated **Butler's Wharf** warehouse complex.

Southeast of here, the historic borough of **Greenwich** has no need of embellishments to its enduring attractions, which include the excellent **National Maritime Museum**, the **Royal Observatory**, the *Cutty Sark* and *Gypsy Moth IV*.

DON'T MISS

*** Museum of the Moving Image: at the South Bank Centre, where cinema comes to life and you can play at being on TV.
*** The Globe Theatre: which has risen from the ashes in an authentic recreation of Shakespeare's original auditorium.
*** Boat trips: down the Thames to explore several fascinating attractions in **Greenwich**.
** Southwark: walk over Tower Bridge to visit a clutch of unusual museums and attractions.

Opposite: *The Imperial War Museum has fascinating displays.*

THE SOUTH BANK
South Bank Centre ★★

Facing the Victoria Embankment and Charing Cross station on the other side of the Thames, the South Bank Centre is a massive arts and entertainment complex covering some 11ha (27 acres). Its grimy, block-like concrete exterior and windswept concrete walkways are loathed by many, but the vast range of arts, music, drama, film and poetry events staged within it make the South Bank Centre one of the main cultural hubs of the city. The centre developed after the 1951 Festival of Britain, a post-war effort to boost morale, with the South Bank Exhibition as its centrepiece, constructed on wasteland on the banks of the Thames.

The oldest building in the complex is the **Royal Festival Hall** (RFH), built in 1951 with a sound-proofed auditorium suspended above the foyer. The RFH is one of the capital's main concert venues with the London Philharmonic as its resident orchestra. Jazz, dance and ballet are also staged here. The other main concert halls are the **Queen Elizabeth Hall** and the more intimate **Purcell Room**. Behind these venues is the **Hayward**

SOUTH BANK EVENTS

For details of performances, exhibitions, films and other special events contact:
- Hayward Gallery (tel: 0171 261-0127);
- Museum of the Moving Image (tel: 0171 928-3535);
- Royal National Theatre (tel: 0171 452-3333);
- Royal Festival Hall (tel: 0171 921-0849);
- National Film Theatre (tel: 0171 928-3232).

Right: *The Royal Festival Hall at the South Bank Centre, built on the site of former warehouses and factories which were destroyed during World War II.*

Gallery (open daily 10:00–18:00, closing 20:00 Tuesday and Wednesday), easily located amidst this concrete jungle by the tall neon sculpture on its roof. The Hayward hosts major classical and contemporary art exhibitions. Downstream, the blockhouse of the **Royal National Theatre** contains three separate performance venues (the Olivier, Lyttelton and Cottesloe theatres) which between them stage a wide variety of productions. Then there is the **National Film Theatre** (NFT), which has two auditoriums where some 2000 films are screened each year, and talks, workshops and lectures are hosted. The London Film Festival is held here every November.

Museum of the Moving Image ★★★

Unless you were visiting the South Bank for a performance or a show at the Hayward, this is probably the only drawcard in the area – and well worth the effort it is too. A series of impressive displays trace the history of cinema and television starting with the earliest optical projectors through cinema during the war, the beginnings of Hollywood, the development of television, to props from **Star Wars**, **King Kong** and much more besides. In the best spirit of cinematic traditions costumed actors are on hand to enlighten visitors on the various exhibits, and you can try your hand at creating a cartoon, reading the news, being interviewed on a set, or even 'flying' like Superman. Alongside the NFT, the museum is open 10:00–18:00 daily.

A REVAMPED SOUTH BANK

There have been many attempts over the years to improve the image of the South Bank, with its drab concrete exterior and windswept walkways. Most recently, Richard Rogers planned to cover it with a wave-like glass roof, but Lottery funding was not forthcoming, so it is back to the drawing board. However, one plan which will probably go ahead is a massive ferris wheel which is being built in Jubilee Gardens for the millennium, offering spectacular views over London. Further east is the Coin Street Development, at the centre of which is the distinctive Oxo Tower, which has been redeveloped to include offices, shops, craft workshops, an exclusive restaurant and a public viewing platform.

Left: *The Museum of the Moving Image (MOMI) offers an interesting day out for all the family as well as research facilities for media students.*

Above: *The attractive Tudor Gatehouse at Lambeth Palace.*

LAMBETH
Imperial War Museum ★★

From the horrors of the trenches of Flanders to hi-tech battles of the Gulf War, the whole range of modern warfare is presented in the Imperial War Museum. The massive main gallery features tanks, V2 rockets, a Spitfire and a Polaris missile. Interactive exhibits include walk-through World War I trenches (complete with mud, rats and simulated shellfire), a recreated Blitz scenario in the bomb-ravaged streets of wartime London, and the new Secret War exhibition. There are also interactive videos and Operation Jericho, a highly realistic flight simulator. Open 10:00–18:00, daily.

Florence Nightingale Museum ★

On a corner of St Thomas's Hospital where the 'Lady with the Lamp' set up the first professional school of nursing, this small but interesting museum charts the life of the indefatigable campaigner, with audiovisual presentations and recreations of the Crimean military hospitals where she earned her reputation as a heroine (her 'white lamp' is also displayed). Open 10:00–16:00, Tuesday–Sunday.

Museum of Garden History ★

Next door to Lambeth Palace, inside the church of St Mary-at-Lambeth (deconsecrated in 1972) are displays on the development of garden design and early plant hunters (such as 17th-century Royal Gardener, John Tradescant, who travelled widely to bring new species back to Britain), as well as antique gardening tools. Outside, there is a period garden with a peculiar memorial to Tradescant and, unexpectedly, the sarcophagus of Captain Bligh of *Mutiny on the Bounty* fame. Open 10:30–16:00 weekdays; 10:30–17:00 Sunday; closed December–February.

LAMBETH PALACE

As Westminster began to emerge as the focus for political and royal power in the 13th century, the clergy decided they had to have a presence nearby, so the Bishop of Winchester built **Southwark Palace** (of which little remains), and the then Archbishop of Canterbury built **Lambeth Palace**, which is still the Archbishop's London residence. This palace is still largely intact, but not open to the public.

SOUTHWARK

Just across the river, Southwark offers many interesting sightseeing possibilities from the famous **Southwark Cathedral** to a variety of historical pubs, such as the George Inn, and unusual museums.

The Globe Theatre ★★★

Completed in 1996, the recreation of one of the world's most famous theatres as it was in its heyday in the early 1600s, is a remarkable new addition to the city's attractions and theatrical venues. The first thatched building in the capital since the Great Fire of London, the Globe features authentic renditions of Shakespeare's works as they were originally performed. The complex also includes an indoor theatre (based on a design by Inigo Jones in 1617), restaurants, and the Shakespeare Globe Exhibition. Open daily 09:00–17:00; visits include a tour of the theatre itself.

Design Museum ★★

This museum, in a converted warehouse just past Butler's Wharf, provides a revealing insight into design as it relates to everyday objects such as cars and furniture. The top floor **Collection Gallery** has themed displays from the permanent collection, and the first floor **Review Gallery** show-cases new products – some not in production yet. Graphics and photographs are displays in the ground floor foyer. Open 11:30–18:00 daily. Tel: (0171) 378-6055 for details of exhibitions.

The London Dungeon ★★

Housed in railway vaults on Tooley Street, the Dungeon is a macabre tour through history. Over 40 exhibits cover gruesome forms of death and torture. Life-size tableaux depict people being boiled, beheaded, hanged, drawn and quartered. Open 10:00– 18:30 daily, last admission 16:30.

> ### THE GLOBE THEATRE
>
> Shakespeare's plays were written for his theatre on the banks of the Thames, known as the 'Wooden O', and it was here that *King Lear*, *Macbeth*, *Hamlet*, *Othello* and many other productions were first staged. It was closed down by the Puritans in 1642. The current recreation is largely due to the American film-maker Sam Wanamaker, who came to London in 1949 expecting to find a Globe Theatre and, disappointed, set about raising funds to rebuild it; he died in 1993, but his vision has finally been realized. A full performance season in the half-covered theatre (which holds an audience of 1500) began in 1997.

Below: *The Globe Theatre, where Shakespeare's plays are performed as they would have been in the 1600s.*

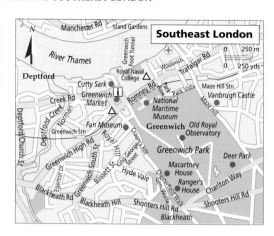

Winston Churchill's Britain at War Experience **

Just down the road from the London Dungeon, this new theme museum effectively conveys the atmosphere of wartime London and how people coped with life during the Blitz (rationing, blackouts and so forth). It starts with a creaking elevator ride into an air-raid shelter and finishes with an impressively realistic mock-up of a bombed-out, rubble-strewn street complete with special effects such as smells and smoke. Open daily 10:00– 17:30 (April–Sept); 10:00–16:30 (Oct–March).

HMS *Belfast* **

The largest surviving battle cruiser from the Second World War, **HMS *Belfast*** is now a floating museum, permanently moored upstream from Tower Bridge. This huge and complex warship (which carried 800 crew) has seven decks and you can explore all of it, from the bridge down to the engine and boiler rooms. Open daily 10:00–18:00; 10:00–17:00 in winter.

Bramah Tea and Coffee Museum *

It's a shame that this museum's rambling displays on the history of tea and coffee are not organized logically. Nonetheless, there are some interesting items to be seen among the 1000 teapots and coffee-makers. Open daily.

GREENWICH

One of London's most attractive villages, Greenwich makes a pleasant excursion along the Thames. As you arrive you will be greeted by the magnificent riverside view of the Royal Naval College, with the Queen's House set in the middle.

National Maritime Museum ***

Britain's seafaring history (from the 15th century to the Falklands War) is the main theme of this museum. One of the focal points is a gallery featuring **20th Century Sea Power** but one of the most exciting exhibits is the new **Nelson Gallery**, which brings together material on the private and public lives of Admiral Lord Nelson – including the coat he was wearing at the Battle of Trafalgar (with the hole made by the musket ball which killed him, and the ball itself – salvaged by the ships' surgeon – alongside). Turner's *Battle of Trafalgar* is another highlight, with a taped commentary explaining why the painting caused so much controversy. The most recent addition to the museum is a new interactive **All Hands** gallery where you can try out seafaring skills (including piloting a ship out of Dover harbour in a realistic computer simulation). Open 10:00–17:00, daily.

The Queen's House **

Originally designed by Inigo Jones for Anne of Denmark, the Queen's House was completed in 1638 as a gift from Charles I for his French wife, Henrietta Maria, who called it her 'House of Delights'. The main rooms have been restored to how they were, with seperate apartments for the King and the Queen. Open daily from 10:00–17:00.

EXPLORING GREENWICH

Greenwich can be reached by boat from Charing Cross, by train or bus from Westminster or Tower piers, or by taking the Docklands Light Railway and walking through the foot tunnel under the Thames. **Greenwich Royal Park,** which was once the private hunting grounds of kings and queens, is a lovely area to wander around. Daily **guided walks,** at 12:15 and 14:15, leave from the **Tourist Information Centre,** (46 Greenwich Church Street). Tel: (0181) 858-6376 for details. There is an excellent arts and crafts market in **Bosun's Yard** (daily in summer, weekends in winter).Tel: (0181) 293-3110 for times.

Below: *Wren's Royal Naval College buildings at Greenwich, with the Old Royal Observatory rising up behind.*

During the early 19th century most parts of Britain ran on different time zones, which was fine during the days of stage-coach travel but it made the timetables of the newly-emerging rail network particularly confusing. From 1852 London time was adopted as standard, but clocks still showed both local and London time; this continued until 1884 when Greenwich Mean Time (GMT) was adopted as the standard by which not just Britain but the whole world set its clocks. An international convention placed Longitude 0 degs (the imaginary line joining the North and South Poles) at Greenwich, and by standing on this Meridian (an illuminated line on the ground) at the Old Royal Observatory you are straddling the eastern and western hemispheres. The red time ball on top of Flamsteed House (the old observatory) is raised and dropped every day – as it has been for over a century – at 13:00 as a time signal to shipping on the River Thames.

The Old Royal Observatory ★★

Built in 1676 for Charle's II's Royal Astronomer, the Old Royal Observatory sits atop the hill in Greenwich Park on the Greenwich Meridian line, and features an interesting display on time and astronomy, with old telescopes and other instruments. One of the exhibits is the first marine chronometer, probably 'the most important timepiece ever made' since it enabled ships to calculate longitude, and so navigate accurately for the first time. Open 10:00–17:00 daily.

There is a stunning view across to Docklands, with the Royal Naval College buildings, designed by Wren, in the foreground. Behind the Observatory and the southern edge of the Park is the open expanse of Blackheath, popular for kite flying, and with two pubs (the Hare and Billet and the Princess of Wales) on its southern perimeter.

Cutty Sark and *Gypsy Moth IV* ★★

On board the *Cutty Sark* are many interesting features, including the original gilded teak fittings, the rigging on its three masts, and a collection of maritime memorabilia. The below-decks area houses colourful figureheads, and some cabins above contain tableaux of what ship life was like. Built on the Clyde in 1869, the *Cutty Sark* was one of the last tea clippers, fast sailing ships which competed each year to bring the first of the new tea crop back from China. Open 10:00–17:00 daily.

On the same wharf the *Gypsy Moth IV* looks tiny

alongside the *Cutty Sark*'s 50m (164ft) masts. This 16m (52ft) ketch was the first to be sailed aroundthe world single-handed when Francis Chichester made his record-breaking circumnavigation in 1966–67.

On his return, he was knighted by her Majesty the Queen with Sir Francis Drake's sword. *Gypsy Moth IV* is currently closed to the public.

Left: *The Thames Barrier at Woolwich.*
Opposite: *Greenwich Park, with the Royal Naval College in the background.*

WOOLWICH
The Thames Barrier *

London has always lived with the threat of flooding from the Thames, an event which occurs far more frequently than might be expected.

A flood barrier was first proposed in the 19th century, but it wasn't until the 1980s that one was actually built – a unique and impressive structure it is too, with its ten massive stainless steel gates, each weighing 3700 tonnes, which take half-an-hour to be raised or lowered. They have been used to prevent floods more than 20 times since being completed, and are tested every month (for schedules, tel: (0181) 305-4188).

There are good views of the structure – the largest movable flood barrier in the world – from the visitors centre which has information on their construction and operation. Open 10:00–17:00, Monday–Friday, 10:30–17:30, weekends. For a clear view of the barrier from the river, take a boat trip from Greewich.

Woolwich Railway Museum*

The Railway Museum in North Woolwich is a must for all railway enthusiasts. It is located at the old Railway Station and depicts the history of the Great Eastern Railway, founded in 1839. There are also a number of restored steam engines on display. Open Monday–Friday 10:00–17:00; Sunday 14:00–17:00.

MILITARY WOOLWICH

Woolwich has a long history as a military depot, starting with the creation of the **Royal Dockyards** in 1513 by Henry VIII. Both Sir Walter Raleigh and Captain Cook set out on their historic voyages of discovery from the docks here, which eventually closed in 1869. Alongside the now derelict docks are the abandoned buildings of the **Royal Arsenal** (where gunpowder was manufactured in the 17th century), whilst nearby there are also the **Royal Artillery Barracks** and the **Old Royal Military Academy**.

9
Nearby Excursions

There are many interesting places to visit just a short distance from the centre of London. **Chiswick**, in West London, is a quaint village-like area, with riverside pubs – such as the City Barge at Strand-on-the-Green, dating from 1484, and reached from Kew Bridge (near the Steam Museum) – and the splendours of **Chiswick House** all within easy walking distance.

As the River Thames loops its way southwards, it passes through **Kew** and **Richmond**, affluent suburbs which have enjoyed Royal patronage from the 12th century, when palaces were built here on the riverbanks. The fabulous **Kew Gardens** is one of the chief legacies of the old royal estates, as is the walled **Richmond Park**, where herds of deer roam among the bracken and coppices. Other attractions include stately mansions such as **Syon House** and **Osterley House**.

Still further to the southwest is **Hampton Court**, one of the greatest of the Royal palaces, with wonderfully opulent rooms hidden away behind its red-brick exterior. The magnificent gardens add to the allure of this vast palace, which is well worth the 20km (12½ mile) journey out from the centre of town.

And, of course, no visit to London would be complete without a trip to **Windsor Castle**, although it is some 40km (25 miles) from the city centre. A palpable sense of nearly a thousand years of history pervades this towered and turreted complex on a hilltop above the Thames. You can tour the royal apartments and view the superb Royal Collection.

DON'T MISS

*** Hampton Court Palace and **Windsor Castle:** royal residences teeming with history.
*** Kew Gardens: visit the lush Palm House as well as the Temperate House.
** Syon and **Osterley House:** lordly riverbank mansions.
** Richmond Park: walk, ride a bicycle or have a picnic in these vast royal hunting grounds.
* Chiswick: traditional pub lunches, overlooking the Thames riverside.

Opposite: *Henry VIII's magnificent Tudor palace at Hampton Court.*

Below: *Walpole House at Chiswick. Its riverside village atmosphere, pubs and archi-tecture make Chiswick an enjoyable excursion choice.*

CHISWICK

Its pleasant riverside location makes the village of Chiswick a good finishing point for a walk along the banks of the Thames, with the attractive **Chiswick Mall** boasting a series of grand houses overlooking the houseboats moored on the tidal reaches. The atmo-spheric **Church Lane** was the original medieval high street, with the graveyard of the church of **St Nicholas** (which has a 15th-century tower) containing the graves of painters J M Whistler and William Hogarth. **Hogarth's House** is just a short stroll away, with many of his famous satirical engravings – which so enraged the establishment at the time – displayed inside. Open 13:00–17:00 Tuesday–Friday (16:00 winter); 13:00–18:00 Saturday– Sunday (17:00 winter).

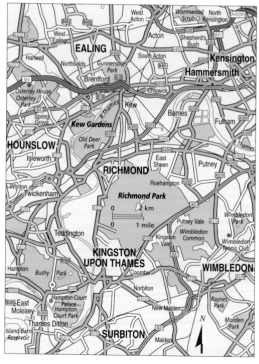

Chiswick House **

The highlight of Chiswick is undoubtedly Chiswick House, a classical, Palladian-style villa built by arts patron Lord Burlington in 1729. It was designed as a gallery for his art collection and as a setting for meeting his coterie, which included leading intellectuals of the time such as Alexander Pope and Jonathan Swift, and composers such as Handel. The inside of the house contains an historical exhibition, the Earl's library, several richly-decorated ceilings and a special domed octagonal hall at its centre, where paintings and sculptures were once displayed. The house is surrounded by superb gardens, complete with Roman statuary and an Ionic temple overlooking a grassy amphitheatre with a pond at its centre. Open 10:00–18:00 daily, 1 March–21 October; 10:00–16:00 Wed–Sun, 22 October–1 March.

Kew Bridge Steam Museum *

This old Victorian water works features a massive Steam Hall with four monster Cornish beam engines, maintained by volunteers and fired up at weekends – which is evidently the best time to visit if you're a steam enthusiast. There's also a miniature steam railway and displays on the history of water power. Open 11:00–17:00, daily.

Above: *Built around a central octagonal room, Chiswick House is a classic example of Palladian-style architecture.*
Below: *Chiswick Mall and Church, seen from the Thames.*

Right: *Osterley House, a fine example of neoclassical Robert Adam architecture.*
Opposite: *Victoria Regis water lilies in the Princess of Wales Conservatory at Kew Gardens.*

SYON AND OSTERLEY
Syon House **

One of several mansions renovated by the talented designer Robert Adam in the late 1700s, this contains one of London's most exuberant period interiors. The most interesting rooms are the splendid Great Hall, with Doric columns and statuary, the Ante Room and Dining Room, the silk-hung Red Drawing Room, and a Long Gallery; the walls are hung with works by Gainsborough, Reynolds, Van Dyck and others. Open 11:00–17:00, Wednesday–Sunday and Bank holidays, April–October. The outside gardens and conservatory were designed by Capability Brown. Open 10:00–18:00 daily. The grounds also have a trout fishery, garden centre, and **Butterfly House.** Open 10:00–17:00 daily (closes 15:30 in winter).

Osterley House and Park *

One of the last great country houses with an intact estate within the London area, Osterley House is approached through the park along an avenue of towering chestnut trees, and past an ornamental lake with a pagoda. The neoclassical house is one of the finest remaining examples of the work of Robert Adam, and the richly decorated interiors – particularly those in the south wing – contain furniture by Adam, and paintings by Reynolds. Open 14:00–17:00, Wednesday–Saturday, April–October; 11:00–17:00, Sunday. The park is open 09:00 until sunset.

FLOWERING SEASONS AT KEW

- **January:** Camellias, shrubs, alpines and heathers.
- **February:** Crocuses and snowdrops.
- **March:** Daffodils and cherry blossom.
- **April:** Magnolias, tulips, spring bedding.
- **May:** Bluebells, azaleas and lilac.
- **June:** Roses, rhododendrons, chestnut trees.
- **July & August:** Giant waterlily, summer bedding, scented plants.
- **September:** Summer bulbs, start of autumn colour.
- **October:** Late-flowering crocuses, cyclamens.
- **November:** The last of the autumn foliage.
- **December:** Strawberry trees and holly.

KEW
Kew Gardens ★★★

Covering 900ha (2224 acres) on the banks of the Thames between Richmond and Kew, the Royal Botanic Gardens is a fascinating place to visit. It houses one of the greatest collections of plants and plant material in the world, and is a major research centre for the economic and medicinal uses of plants. Kew Gardens also boasts four of the largest glasshouses in the world.

The main entrance to the Gardens (open 09:30 till dusk, daily) is on Lichfield Road at the Victoria Gate, where you should pick up a map at the Visitor Centre before setting off to explore the Gardens. Almost directly opposite is the magnificent **Palm House**, a masterpiece of Victorian engineering in iron and glass. Nearby is the **Waterlily House**, Kew's most humid environment, where sacred lotus bloom in summer. To the west of here is the elegant **Temperate House**, the largest of Kew's glasshouses and a superb setting for many exotic species, citrus fruits, and the world's largest indoor plant (the Chilean Wine Palm). The new **Evolution House**, behind it, traces the development of plant life on the planet over the last 3500 million years.

Other highlights – of which there are many – within the gardens include a towering Pagoda (Kew's most distinctive landmark), the Marianne North Gallery (which houses 832 botanical paintings by this talented Victorian artist), Queen Charlotte's Cottage (once a Royal summer house), and the recently built Princess of Wales Conservatory. One of the least visited royal residences in London (and the smallest in the country), is the intimate **Kew Palace** tucked away on the north side of the gardens; George III and Queen Charlotte used it as their family retreat from 1802–1818. Open 11:00–17:30, daily, April–October.

> ### RESEARCH AT KEW
>
> **Kew Gardens**
> ● is primarily a scientific research centre and amongst its 500 staff has botanists collaborating on projects in 50 different countries;
> ● grows one in eight of all flowering plants;
> ● carries out research on over six million preserved plants;
> ● contains over 1000 threatened species, and 13 which have become extinct in their native habitat;
> ● safeguards more than 80,000 plant products used by mankind;
> ● preserves seeds from more than 3500 plant species;
> ● has a library of more than 750,000 books, journals and plant illustrations.

Right: *A view of the Thames
from Richmond. Easily accessible from the city centre,
Richmond, with its famous
park, beautiful buildings and
riverside location, has a great
deal to offer visitors.*
Opposite: *Riverboats at
Hampton Court.*

RICHMOND

This riverside town's main attraction is its enormous
Park (*see* below), but there are other sights nearby which
are of interest. Between the modern high street and the
Thames lies **Richmond Green**, a lovely square surrounded by Queen Anne and Georgian houses. On the
southwest corner a Tudor gateway is all that remains of
Richmond Palace, dating back to the 12th century but
extensively rebuilt by the Tudors. A famous view,
embracing the Thames Valley and no less than six coun-
ties, is the main reward for climbing **Richmond Hill**
behind the town.

Richmond Park **

Beyond Richmond Hill stretches the huge expanse of
Richmond Park, created by Charles I who hunted here
and enclosed it within a 16km (10 mile) long wall (still
there today) in the 17th century. At 1000ha (2471 acres) it
is easily the largest city park in Europe, and features
rolling grasslands interspersed with coppices, woodland
(mostly oak, beech and chestnut) and ponds. Much of
this is natural wilderness, apart from the landscaped
plantations of rhododendron and azaleas, which provide
gorgeous displays in the spring. Sizeable herds of red
and fallow deer roam all over the park, and twitchers
will also find plenty of birdlife (particularly in **Sidmouth
Wood**, which is a bird sanctuary).

HAMPTON COURT PALACE

Set in 24ha (59 acres) of landscaped gardens and parklands on the banks of the River Thames, Hampton Court is probably the most dazzling of all the royal palaces in England. Of all the monarchs who have lived here it is most closely associated with Henry VIII, and today the tapestry of court life in Tudor times is vividly brought to life by costumed actors in this rambling, turreted building.

Entering the **palace** you should first explore the three **courtyards**, namely the Base Court, the Clock Court, and the Fountain Court.

Retrace your steps to the Base Court to **Henry VIII's State Apartments**, where the Great Hall has an ornate double-hammerbeam roof – Shakespeare's theatrical players performed here under Elizabeth I. Other major rooms include the Great Watching Chamber, the Haunted Gallery, and the Royal Chapel. Within the **Queen's Apartments** the most impressive rooms are the Queen's Drawing Room, the Queen's Gallery, and the Queen's bedroom. Within the **King's Apartments** (which were built for William III), don't miss the 3000-piece display of armoury in the King's Guard Chamber. The prodigious consumption of the Royal Court is vividly brought to life in the massive **Tudor Kitchens**, which have recently been restored to show preparations for a feast day in 1542. Open 10:15–18:00, Monday, 09:30–18:00, Tuesday–Sunday, March–October; 10:15–16:30, Monday, 09:30–16:30, Tuesday–Sunday, October–March.

HAMPTON HISTORY

Hampton Court Palace was originally built by Cardinal Wolsey, Henry VIII's rebellious chancellor, as an ecclesiastical abode. When Henry VIII asked him why he needed such a grand home he made the mistake of replying that it was 'to show how noble a palace a subject may offer to his sovereign'. When he fell from royal favour in 1529 Henry VIII took him up on his offer and moved in, considerably altering and enlarging the palace. Subsequent monarchs used it as a weekend retreat from London (Charles II's private shortcut to the palace was Chelsea's King's Road), with the most significant additions after the Tudors' reign being made by William and Mary, who hired Sir Christopher Wren to rebuild the south and east wings and add the Banqueting Hall.

MUSIC AT HAMPTON COURT

If you're visiting during June it's well worth catching a performance during the **Hampton Court Palace Festival of Music, Opera and Dance**. Founded in 1993, the festival features top-flight international performers (such as José Carreras, Dame Kiri Te Kanawa and Yehudi Menuhin) in the alfresco setting of the Tudor court, with an especially long interval so that the audience can picnic amidst the yew trees and canals of the great Fountain Gardens.

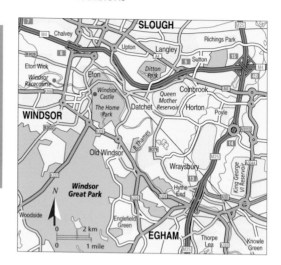

THE CHANGING OF THE GUARD AT WINDSOR

The Changing of the Guard at Windsor takes place at 11:00 daily in summer (alternate days in winter), with the Guard, usually accompanied by a band, marching through the town up to the Castle.
When the Queen is in residence, the Regimental Band is also on parade.

WINDSOR

Below: *Guardsmen outside St George's Chapel, Windsor Castle.*

The network of cobbled streets of Windsor's Old Town are choc-a-bloc with antiques and souvenir shops and feature several interesting buildings, including **Burford House** (where Charles II housed his mistress Nell Gwynne), and the **Guildhall**, standing on pillars in the High Street, which was finished by Sir Christopher Wren.

Windsor Castle ★★★

The oldest and largest inhabited castle in England and the official weekend residence of the Queen, Windsor Castle's imposing battlements and turrets dominate the town from its hilltop site, 40km (25 miles) from central London.

Originally a timber and earth stronghold built by William the Conqueror, the castle steadily grew in importance during Norman and Plantagenet times and was rebuilt in stone by Henry II. The present design of the castle was influenced by George III and his son, George IV, and it was the latter that added a bigger **Round Tower** – one of the castle's most distinguishing features – and many of the state apartments.

Entering the castle you go through the Middle Ward, with the Round Tower in its centre. Continue past the Winchester Gates to the North Terrace, where there are superb views over the Chiltern Hills and Eton College. Here is the entrance to the **State Apartments**, badly damaged in a major fire in 1992 but now fully restored to their former splendour. Amid the gilded ceilings and ornate furnishings are several important works by Rubens, Rembrandt and Van Dyck as well as superb Gobelin tapestries. Don't miss the exquisite **Queen Mary's Dolls House**, an extraordinary creation which took three years to complete. Designed by Edwin Lutyens in 1920, the house has working plumbing, lifts, and electricity. Nearby is the **Gallery**, which features themed exhibitions from the extensive Royal Collection of paintings, sculpture and objets d'art. Open 10:00–16:00, daily, March–October; 10:00–15:00, daily, November–February.

Passing through the Lower Ward you reach **St George's Chapel**, one of the finest ecclesiastical buildings in England, begun in 1475 by Edward IV. Ten monarchs (including Henry VIII and his favourite wife, Jane Seymour) are buried here; one of the best times to visit the chapel is when the choir is singing evensong (17:15 daily).

> **GETTING THERE**
>
> Windsor is around 45 minutes by train from central London, with frequent services from Waterloo to Windsor Riverside and from Paddington to Windsor Central (change at Slough). Both stations are close to the town centre. For details on train times or other information contact the Information Centre, 24 High Street, tel: (01753) 743-900.

Overleaf: *The dome of St Paul's, dominating the City skyline by night.* **Below:** *Windsor Castle viewed from the Long Walk.*

Eton *

A short walk takes you from Windsor to Eton, home of one of Britain's most famous 'public' schools, where pupils wear a characteristic uniform of top hat and morning coat. Over the years, Eton has educated many of the country's prime ministers and top politicians.

London at a Glance

BEST TIMES TO VISIT

London's unpredictable weather (see p. 7) means that it is always best to pack an umbrella and raincoat. Despite seasonal fluctuations, the city's climate is essentially temperate and there may be sunny days almost throughout the year. **October–April** are probably the least crowded, with the peak (long queues at major attractions) July–August. Prices are the same year-round, but book summer accommodation well in advance.

GETTING THERE

By Air: There are direct flights to the UK from all major cities. The main airports for international flights are **Heathrow**, **Gatwick** and **Stansted**.
• **Heathrow:** 24km (14 miles) west of central London. The fastest way to the city centre is by Heathrow Express into Paddington, which takes 15 minutes and runs every 15 minutes from 05:00–23:45. The **Piccadilly Underground Line is cheaper, takes** 30–50 minutes and runs from 07:00–00:30 Mon–Sat, 07:00–23:30 Sun. The **Airbus** takes 1 hour. Route A1 takes you to Victoria via Earl's Court and Kensington. Route A2 goes to King's Cross via Bayswater and Bloomsbury. **Taxis** from Heathrow are expensive (£35 one-way).
• **Gatwick:** 50km (30 miles) south of London. The **Gatwick Express** runs from the airport to Victoria Station (30 min), departing every 15 mins. **Flightline 777** coaches depart hourly for Victoria Coach Station (60–90 min).
• **Stansted:** 60km (37 miles) northeast is London's newest airport. **Stansted Express** runs to Liverpool Street station (45 min), departing every ½hr.
• **London City Airport:** In London Docklands, mostly used by commuters to and from Paris, Brussels, Amsterdam and other European cities. **Shuttle bus** to Liverpool Street Station (25 min) every 20 minutes, or to connect with the **Docklands Light Railway**, Canary Wharf.

By Road and Sea: Visitors from Europe may choose **ferry services** from the Channel ports or the **Channel Tunnel**. Services through the tunnel include Le Shuttle for drivers and **Eurostar** trains for passengers running direct from Paris and Brussels with connecting services from other European departure points.

GETTING AROUND

London has an extensive public transport system: red double-decker **buses** (many are now seen in different liveries), **black taxis**, and the **Underground** trains (the 'tube'). Congested streets mean that the tube remains quickest and most practicable.
The Underground: There are 11 lines, covering most districts except south of the Thames. Trains run 05:30–24:00 (07:30–23:30 Sundays); tickets available from machines or booths. The tube operates on a zone system, with a standard fare for all stations within a zone: the more zones you cross the more expensive the ticket will be. Travellers without tickets face fines of £10.
Buses: Travelling by **bus** has the bonus of sightseeing from the top deck. Most buses run 06:00–24:00; **night buses** (N prefix before the route number) run 24:00–06:00. There are two types of bus stop: compulsory ones (the sign has a white background) and request stops (with a red background). Fares operate on a zone system similar to the tube. On most buses you pay the driver on entry, but on some older Routemaster buses (with an open rear platform) a conductor will collect fares.
Taxis: London's famous **black cabs** (nowadays often coloured or covered in sponsors' adverts) run on meters according to the distance travelled and time of day. Taxis can be hailed on the street (when the yellow TAXI sign is lit, it means they are available). Radio Taxis tel: (0171) 272-0272). Computer Cabs (0171) 286-0286. **Mini cabs** are cheaper but the driver's street knowledge is less professional; always agree a price before setting off. They are not allowed to pick up passengers in the street.

London at a Glance

The West End
LUXURY

Brown's Hotel, 30–34 Albemarle Street, W1, tel: (0171) 493-6020. Popular, old-fashioned; furnished with antiques, refurbished 1995.
Claridge's, Brook Street, W1, tel: (0171) 629-8860. Favourite with royalty and superstars. It's expensive, but service is good.
The Dorchester, 53 Park Lane, W1, tel: (0171) 629-8888. One of London's landmark hotels, overlooking Hyde Park, popular with movie stars.
The London Hilton, 22 Park Lane, W1, tel: (0171) 493-8000. Excellent views of Hyde Park; impeccable service and decor.
The Ritz, 150 Piccadilly, W1 tel: (0171) 493-8181. Steeped in history and a tourist attraction in its own right, the Ritz features opulent Louis XVI decor with the west-facing rooms (overlooking Green Park) the best ones to book.

MID-RANGE

The Goring, 17 Beeston Place, SW1, tel: (0171) 396-9000. Well-located, family-run hotel with elegant public rooms and spacious en-suite bedrooms.

Bloomsbury and Covent Garden
LUXURY

The Savoy, Strand, WC2, tel: (0171) 836-4343. Synonymous with top service and luxury; spacious rooms decorated in art deco. Good fitness centre.

MID-RANGE

Hazlitt's, 6 Frith Street, W1, tel: (0171) 434-1771. Period-style rooms in 18th-century home of essayist William Hazlitt.

BUDGET

Ruskin, 23–24 Montague Street, WC1, tel: (0171) 636-7388. Excellent location in Bloomsbury, good value.

West and Southwest London
LUXURY

Blakes, 33 Roland Gardens, SW7, tel: (0171) 370-6701. Popular with celebrities. Glamorous interiors and suites.
The Beaufort, 33 Beaufort Gardens, SW3, tel: (0171) 584-5252. Stylish hotel with large, modern rooms and good value for money.

MID-RANGE

The Gallery Hotel, 8–10 Queensberry Place, SW7, tel: (0171) 915-0000. Traditional Georgian with spacious suites.
The Pelham, 15 Cromwell Place, SW7, tel: (0171) 589-8288. Small, comfortable; with individually decorated rooms.

BUDGET

Amsterdam Hotel, 7 Trebovir Road, SW5. Tel: (0171) 370-5084. Comfortable B&B near Earl's Court, all rooms with en-suite facilities.
Hotel 167, 167 Old Brompton Rd, SW5, tel: (0171) 373-0672. Slightly upmarket B&B, all rooms with en suite facilities.

The City, the East End and Docklands
Barbican Hotel, Central Street, EC1, tel: (0171) 251-1565. Modern hotel, close to Barbican Arts Centre and City.
Tower Thistle Hotel, St Katherine's Way, E1, tel: (0171) 481-2575. Modern; superbly situated next to Tower Bridge.

North London
MID-RANGE

La Gaffe, 107–111 Heath Street, NW3, tel: (0171) 435-4941. Good location near the Heath, attractive rooms.

BUDGET

Hampstead Village Guesthouse, 2 Kemplay Rd, NW3, tel: (0171) 435-8679. Excellent value for money.

South and Southeast London
BUDGET

The Windmill, Clapham Common Southside, tel: (0181) 673-4578. On the edge of Clapham Common, with few competitors; reasonable value.

Further afield
MID-RANGE

Petersham Hotel, Nightingale Lane, Richmond tel: (0181) 940-7471. Close to Richmond Park; views over the Thames.

BUDGET

The Plough, 42 Christchurch Rd, East Sheen, SW14, tel: (0181) 876-7833. Charming traditional pub; cosy rooms.

London at a Glance

WHERE TO EAT

Whitehall and Westminster
Tate Gallery Restaurant,
Tate Gallery, Millbank, SW1,
tel: (0171) 887-8877. Spacious,
imposing setting, with changing
menu and excellent desserts.
The Stockpot, 40 Panton
Street, London SW1, tel:
(0171) 839-5142. Cheap and
cheerful – perfect for a quick,
filling and inexpensive meal
before the theatre or cinema.

The West End
Tiddy Dols, 55 Shepherd
Market, W1, tel: (0171)
499-2357. Traditional English
food served in quaint
Georgian building.
Gay Hussar, 2 Greek Street,
W1, tel: (0171) 437-0973.
Famous and long-established
Hungarian restaurant.
China City, White Bear Yard,
25A Lisle Street, WC2, tel:
(0171) 734-3388. Tucked
away in a courtyard with a
bright interior; popular for the
extensive dim sum menu.
dell'Ugo, 56 Frith Street, W1,
tel: (0171) 734-8300. Inexpensive café on the ground floor
and expensive two-tier restaurant above; Mediterranean fare
at this popular Soho spot.
Hard Rock Café, 150 Old
Park Lane, W1, tel: (0171)
629-0382. Queues are one of
the drawbacks of this famous
burger joint decorated with
rock memorabilia; high prices
but usually worth the wait.
Planet Hollywood, Trocadero,
13 Coventry St, W1, tel: (0171)

287-1000. Busy theme restaur-
ant with enormous portions.
Rock & Sole Plaice, 47 Endell
St, WC2, tel: (0171) 836-3785.
Limited but reliable fish & chip
menu; central location.
Sports Café, 80 Haymarket,
SW1, tel: (0171) 839-8300.
Catch 150 satellite channels
on 120 TV sets; restaurant,
three bars and a dance floor.

**Bloomsbury and
Covent Garden**
The Savoy Grill, Savoy Hotel,
The Strand, WC2, tel: (0171)
836-4343. Fine surroundings;
impeccable service; food served
from silver: dishes are sometimes unimaginative, but the
desserts are wonderful.
Simpson's in the Strand, 100
Strand, WC2, tel: (0171) 836-
9112. Very traditional; waiters
wheeling out silver platters of
beef and the like. Excellent puddings and breakfasts.
Cork & Bottle, 44-46
Cranbourne Street, WC2, tel:
(0171) 734-7807. Popular wine
bar serves food and has a good
choice of wine, well located for
cinemas and theatres.

**West and
Southwest London**
Bibendum, Michelin House, 81
Fulham Rd, SW3, tel: (0171)
581-5817. Classy, eclectic cuis-
ine in delightful old Michelin
building. Pricey, but worth it.
Chutney Mary, 535 King's Rd,
SW10, tel: (0171) 351-3113.
Best of 'British Raj' cooking and
regional Indian dishes.

La Gavroche, 43 Upper Brook
Street, W1, tel: (0171) 408-
0881. One of London's top
restaurants, famous for the
high standard of its classic
French cuisine.

North London
Belgo Noord, 72 Chalk Farm
Road, NW1, tel: (0171)
267-0718. Amusing decor;
inexpensive and generous portions of Belgian favourites; but
book in advance.
Quality Chop House,
94 Farringdon Rd, EC1,
tel: (0171) 837-5093.
Once a Victorian café, now
moving with the times (with
Mediterranean dishes) but still
serves traditional British nosh.
Sea Shell, 49–51 Lisson Grove,
NW1, tel: (0171) 723-8703.
Famous fish-and-chippie.
Upper Street Fish Shop, 324
Upper Street, N1, tel; (0171)
359-1401. Small and cheerful,
superb fish soup.

**The City, the East End
and Docklands**
The Hothouse, 78–80
Wapping Lane, E1, tel: (0171)
488-4797. Converted spice
warehouse; good value food.

**South and
Southeast London**
Butler's Wharf Chop House,
Butler's Wharf, 36E Shad
Thames, SE1, tel: (0171) 403-
3403. Fabulous views of Tower
Bridge from Terence Conran's
riverfront restaurant. Traditional
British food at its best.

London at a Glance

Le Pont de la Tour, Butler's Wharf, 36D Shad Thames, SE1, tel: (0171) 403-8403. Another Conran outpost, overlooking the river. Attentive service, exhaustive wine list, accent on seafoods.

Further afield
Pissarro's, 1,3 & 5 Kew Green, Richmond, tel: (0181) 948-2049. Wine bar serves imaginative hot and cold food.

WHERE TO SHOP

Napoleon dubbed the English a 'nation of shop-keepers' and London has something for everyone, whatever your tastes or your budget, from grand department stores to speciality shops or bargain-basement market stalls.

Opening hours vary between 09:00, 09:30 & 10:00 – 17:30, 18:00 or 19:00 Mon–Sat and noon to 18:00 Sun.

Late-night shopping varies from area to area (in Kensington High Street, Oxford Street and Covent Garden it is on Thursdays; in Knightsbridge and Chelsea it's Wednesdays) with shops open until 19:00 or 20:00. Many shops are also open longer hours in the month before Christmas.

Prices are considerably reduced during the two major **sales** periods, with the winter sales – the biggest event – running from just after Christmas until early February, and the summer sales starting in June or July.

Most of the large shops and stores accept **credit cards** (the exceptions are Marks & Spencer and John Lewis), but **traveller's cheques** are not commonly accepted as a form of payment. Overseas visitors can sometimes claim back **sales tax** (VAT, or Value Added Tax) on goods purchased (see **Money Matters**, p. 122).

London has so many hundreds of shops that it would take a whole book to list them all; this run down covers some of the main shopping areas.

Oxford Street and Surrounds
Almost a mile long, **Oxford Street** may be one of the most famous shopping streets in the capital but Londoners tend to view it as a rather tawdry area full of cut-price jeans shops and rather tacky souvenirs: this is particularly true in the part to the east of Oxford Circus, whereas to the west it is slightly more upmarket. Oxford Street is home to major chains and department stores such as Selfridges, Marks & Spencer, John Lewis, Next, Debenhams and British Home Stores, as well as mega-media stores such as HMV and Virgin.

To the north of Oxford Street, **St Christopher's Place** features numerous designer outlets, whilst on the opposite side **South Molton Street** is another busy area for fashion

boutiques. Leading off Oxford Street, **Bond Street** and **New Bond Street** feature quality fashions, haute couture, art galleries, jewellery (including Asprey's) and antique shops. Leading down from Oxford Circus to Piccadilly, **Regent Street** is home to Liberty's department store, Laura Ashley, Hamley's toyshop, several crystal and china shops, a Disney store and Warner Bros, and classic British clothing shops such as Aquascutum, Jaeger and Austin Reed. Off Regent Street, **Carnaby Street** was famous during the 'Swinging Sixties' but is now full of tacky souvenir shops.

Running parallel to Regent Street on its west side, **Savile Row** is the place to go for bespoke tailoring.

Piccadilly and St James's
Piccadilly Circus features the indoor shopping complexes of the Trocadero and London Pavilion, as well as Lillywhites, the sports department store, and the massive Tower Records. **Piccadilly** is lined with car showrooms and airline offices but has some famous name shops such as Fortnum and Mason, and Hatchards (books). South of Piccadilly in St James's is **Jermyn Street**, which has numerous small, old-fashioned shops offering exciting finds such as beautiful hand-made shoes, shirts and the like.

London at a Glance

On the north side of Piccadilly, the **Burlington Arcade** is another old-fashioned enclave with good quality shops selling everything from porcelain to antique jewellery, Irish linen and cashmere jumpers.

Knightsbridge, Kensington and Chelsea

One of the most expensive shopping areas in the capital, **Knightsbridge** features numerous classy boutiques and designer fashion shops, as well as world-famous Harrods. **Sloane Street**, with Harvey Nichols and yet more expensive clothing out-lets, leads down into **Sloane Square** and the beginning of **King's Road**. Once one of London's great fashion meccas, King's Road can still hold its own with plenty of trendy designer outlets. **Kensington** has antique shops along **Kensington Church Street**, department stores and clothes boutiques on **Kensington High Street**, and a cluster of fashionable designer outlets in tiny **Brompton Cross**.

Covent Garden and Soho

Covent Garden has a wonderfully eclectic mix of shops, selling virtually everything from designer clothes to arts, crafts, books, antiques and more. To the north of Covent Garden, **Floral Street** is hot on street fashions, while **Neal's Yard** tends to be the focus for rather 'alternative' goods and wholefoods. Alongside the pornographic outlets in **Soho** there are many unusual specialist shops, from continental delicatessens to small record outlets.

Between Soho and Covent Garden, **Charing Cross Road** is synonymous with the book trade, with numerous specialized outlets (for both new and secondhand books), and major bookstores such as Foyles (No. 119) and Waterstones (No. 121).

London has a vast range of markets, rewarding places to browse for crafts, antiques, and bargains of every description among the hordes. Some of the better known ones include **Brick Lane** market (open Sundays 06:00–13:00 near Spitalfields E1); **Bermondsey** (New Caledonian) market (antiques, furniture, bric-a-brac; open Fridays from 05:00); the **Camden Lock Market**, Camden Passage (*see* p. 91); Portobello Road (fruit and vegetables, clothes, antiques, records; open Saturdays); **Greenwich** (bric-a-brac, arts, crafts, clothes; open Saturday and Sunday); and **Petticoat Lane** (clothes, bric-a-brac, and more; open Sundays).

DEPARTMENT STORES

Fortnum and Mason, 181 Piccadilly, W1, tel: (0171) 734-8040. Open 09:30–18:00, Mon–Sat.
Harrods, 87 Brompton Road, SW1, tel: (0171) 730-1234. Open 10:00–18:00, Mon, Tues and Sat; 10:00–19:00, Wed–Fri.
Harvey Nichols, 102–125 Knightsbridge, SW1, tel: (0171) 235-5000. Open 10:00–19:00, Mon, Tues, Thurs–Sat; 10:00– 20:00, Wed; 12:00–18:00, Sun.
John Lewis, 278–306 Oxford Street, W1, tel: (0171) 629-7711. Open 09:30–18:00, Mon, Tues, Wed, Fri; 10:00–20:00, Thurs; 09:00–18:00, Sat.
Liberty, 212–299 Regent Street, W1, tel: (0171) 734-1234. Open 10:00–18:30, Mon–Sat; 10:00–19:30, Thurs.
Marks & Spencer, 458 Oxford Street, W1, tel: (0171) 935-7954. Open 09:00–20:00, Mon–Fri, 09:00 –19:00, Sat; 12:00–18:00 Sun.
Selfridges, 400 Oxford Street, W1, tel: (0171) 629-1234. Open 10:00–19:00, Mon–Wed and 10:00–20:00 Thurs & Fri; 09:30–19:00, Sat and 12:00–18:00, Sun.

TOURS AND EXCURSIONS

One of the great advantages of visiting London is that there are so many other interesting places within a reasonable distance of

London at a Glance

the capital which you can visit for an enjoyable day out, or for a slightly longer stay. With frequent train services from the eight main rail termini in London you don't have to worry about driving either; coaches are another option, with hundreds of services from the Victoria Coach Station daily. Victoria Coach Station, 164 Buckingham Palace Rd, SW1, tel: (0171) 730-3466. The following tour operators offer day-tours from London to all the major tourist destinations, and all use qualified Blue Badge Guides:
Golden Tours
(0171) 233-7030
Evan Evans
(0181) 332-2222
Frames Rickards
(0171) 837-3111
Visitors Sightseeing
(0171) 636-7175.
To the southeast of London, **Canterbury** has long been a place of pilgrimage, with the focal point being the city's magnificent cathedral. The vibrant Sussex coastal town of **Brighton** has a distinguished Regency heritage, excellent shopping and a traditional English seaside pier; the highlight is the newly refurbished Royal Pavilion, the seaside palace of George IV. The coastline of Central Southern England features numerous popular seaside resorts as well as the historic

naval port of **Portsmouth**. Further inland are the ancient cathedral cities of **Winchester** and **Salisbury**. Near Salisbury, the monoliths of **Stonehenge** are one of the country's most famous prehistoric monuments. The West Country features numerous picturesque villages, stately homes and historic monuments. In the county of Avon, **Bath** was first popularized by the Romans as a spa town and with its fine Georgian architecture is considered one of the most elegant towns in the country (it has good shops, too). To the north of Bath, the **Cotswolds** are famous for their pretty, honey-coloured sandstone villages set amongst rolling hills. One of the finest medieval castles in the country is to be found at **Warwick**, to the north of the Cotswolds, while nearby **Stratford-upon-Avon** is, of course, the much-visited birthplace of William Shakespeare. Central England is home to the ancient university town of **Oxford**, where many of the graceful college buildings are open to the public. Further east, the rival university town of **Cambridge** also boasts many fine buildings which can be explored by punt along the river or on foot.

London Regional Transport (LRT) enquiry service for the underground and buses, tel: (0171) 222-1234 (24hrs, 7 days). LRT recorded travel information: tel: (0171) 222-1200.
National train enquiries, tel: (0345) 484-950.
National Express (coach service), tel: (0990) 808-080.
Heathrow airport, tel: (0181) 759-4321.
Gatwick airport, tel: (01293) 53-5353.
London City airport, tel: (0171) 474-5555.
Stansted airport, tel: (01279) 680-500.
Airbus service (to Heathrow), tel: (0181) 400-6655.
Victoria Coach station, tel: (0171) 730-3466.
Docklands Light Railway, tel: (0171) 538-9400.
Radio Taxis (24hr black cab service), tel: (0171) 353-715.
Public Carriage Office, tel: (0171) 230-1631 (for complaints about the taxis); tel: (0171) 833-0996 (for property lost in taxis).
Car Rental:
Avis, tel: (0990) 900-500.
Hertz, tel: (0181) 679-1799.
Europcar, tel: (0345) 222-525.
Hire for Lower, tel: (0171) 491-1111
Disabled: Artsline (free information on access to all arts and entertainment venues and events), tel: (0171) 388-2227

London at a Glance

Holiday Care Service, (advisory service on accommodation for the disabled), tel: (01293) 774-535
LRT Unit for Disabled Passengers (details on access to transport services), tel: (0171) 918-3312.

The London Tourist Board does not run a telephone enquiry service, but there is an automated information service, Visitorcall, with different lines (updated daily) providing information on What's On, Out & About, Where to Take Children, Theatre, Places to Visit, and Accommodation, tel: (0839) 123-456. For a free card listing all services, tel: (0171) 971-0026.
London weather forecast, tel: (0839) 500-951.
Events listings by fax: Annual Events Calendar, tel: (0891) 353-715.
Three-monthly Events Listings, tel: (0831) 353-716. All the above LTB numbers are premium rate lines: calls cost 49p per minute. Fax lines cost 50p per minute.

Double-decker Sightseeing Tours:
• London Pride Sightseeing, with frequent departures from central London points; hop-on, hop-off tickets also available; tel: (01708) 631-122.
• Original London Sightseeing Tours, with departures from Baker Street station, Victoria Station, Marble Arch and Haymarket; tel: (0181) 877-1722.
• The Big Bus Company, hop-on, hop-off service from key tourist spots, tel: (0181) 944-7810.

Driver Guides:
• Flexible itineraries tailored to your interests and personalised service are among the advantages of a driver-guided tour.
• Black Taxi Tours, tel: (0171) 224-2833.
• British Tours, tel: (0171) 734-8734.
• Take a Guide, tel: (0181) 960-0459.

Guide Booking Agencies:
The London registered guides have all undertaken a rigorous training course, after which they are issued with the coveted Blue Badge and photocard licence. The companies listed below can book Blue Badge guides for anything from general sightseeing to special interest tours:
• **Professional Guide Services**, tel: (0181) 874-2745.
• **Tours Guides Ltd**, tel: (0171) 495-5504.
Walking Tours:
• Historical Tours. Daily programme of guided walks on a cultural theme, tel: (0181) 668-4019.
• Original Guided Walks. Mainly focuses on the East End of London and popular 'Jack the Ripper' walks, tel: (0181) 530-8443.
• Original London Walks. London's oldest established walking tour company, which features a varied programme of over 40 walks on different themes, tel: (0171) 264-3978.
• Talking Tours Company. Cassette guided walks featuring a dramatised soundtrack. Copies of the cassettes can be purchased from the LTB's Victoria Tourist Information Centre, tel: (0171) 583-5237.

River/Canal Boat Operators:
• **Bateaux London**, tel: (0171) 925-2215.
• **Catamaran Cruises**, tel: (0171) 839-3572.
• **Circular Cruises**, tel: (0171) 936-2033.

LONDON	J	F	M	A	M	J	J	A	S	O	N	D
AVERAGE TEMP. °F	40	40	44	49	55	61	64	64	59	52	46	42
AVERAGE TEMP. °C	5	5	7	10	13	16	18	18	15	12	8	6
HOURS OF SUN DAILY	1.5	2.2	3.7	5.3	6.6	7.1	6.6	6.2	4.7	3.2	1.7	1.3
RAINFALL ins.	2.1	1.6	1.5	1.5	1.8	1.8	2.2	2.3	1.9	2.2	3	1.9
RAINFALL mm	54	40	37	37	46	45	57	59	49	57	64	48
DAYS OF RAINFALL	15	13	11	12	12	11	12	11	13	13	15	15

Travel Tips

Tourist Information

Overseas offices of the **British Tourist Authority** (BTA) provide a range of leaflets, brochures and free maps and guides, as well as events calendars. Offices can be found in Australia (Sydney), Canada (Toronto), Ireland (Dublin), South Africa (Sandton), New Zealand (Auckland), Singapore, and the USA (New York and Chicago). Main tourist offices within London are the **British Travel Centre** at 1 Lower Regent Street, SW1 (open 09:00–18:30, Mon–Fri; 10:00–16:00, Sat–Sun, tel: (0181) 846-9000) and the **London Tourist Board** at Victoria Station (open 08:00–19:00, reduced hours in winter). Neither centre accepts telephone enquiries. Other LTB information centres are located at **Heathrow Airport** (open 08:00 –18:00, daily), **Liverpool Street Station** and at **Waterloo Station Eurostar Terminal**, all open daily. There is also a **City of London Information Centre** located at St Paul's Churchyard, EC4, tel: (0171) 332-1456/3456

Entry Requirements

No visas are required for travellers from the USA, Japan, Iceland, Austria, Finland, Switzerland, and most European Economic Community (EEC) countries. Citizens of Australia, Canada, New Zealand and most Commonwealth countries (exceptions include Nigeria, Bangladesh, Ghana, India, Sri Lanka and Pakistan) are likewise not required to have visas. The nationals of other countries should apply to the British Embassy or Consulate for visas before leaving home.

Customs

The following restrictions on tax- and duty-free goods apply:
• 200 cigarettes, or 100 cigarillos, or 50 cigars, or 250g (8 ounces) tobacco.
• 2 litres (4 pints) still table wine plus 1 litre (2 pints) spirits or liqueur (over 22% proof), or 2 litres (4 pints) of fortified or sparkling wine (under 22% proof).
• 60ml (2 fluid ounces) perfume plus 250ml (8 fluid ounces) of toilet water.
• Other goods valued at £136. There are restrictions on the import of various other items (firearms, protected species, meat products, etc) and pets such as cats and dogs must undergo six months anti-rabies quarantine. There are no restrictions on the import or export of currency.

Health Requirements

No vaccinations are required.

Money Matters

Currency: British currency is the pound sterling (£), divided into 100 pence (p). Coin denominations are 1p, 2p, 5p, 10p, 20p, 50p, £1 and £2. Notes are in denominations of £5, £10, £20, £50.
Banks: The four major banks, with branches throughout the city are: National Westminster, Barclays, Lloyds and Midland. Standard opening hours are 09:30–15:30, Mon–Fri, but some branches are open until 17:00 on weekdays, and some on Saturday mornings.
Currency Exchange:
Traveller's cheques: Most banks offer currency exchange. You'll need your passport as proof of identity when cashing traveller's cheques. Commission

is usually charged on foreign cheques. Banks usually offer the best rates; outside of banking hours there are numerous **bureaux de change** (08:00–21:00) at stations, airports, and in central tourist areas.

Credit cards: Most hotels, shops and restaurants accept international credit cards such as Access/Mastercard, Visa/Barclaycard, Diners Club and American Express.

VAT: Consumer goods (with major exceptions such as food and books) are subject to a 17.5% sales tax known as VAT (Value Added Tax). Visitors from non-EU countries can recoup VAT on major items but, before you buy, ask for the appropriate form. Customs will validate this when leaving.

Tipping: Service charges are usually included in bills, but many restaurants may also leave a blank space on credit card counterfoils to encourage customers to tip twice! If a tip is not included, waiters expect 10–15%. Hairdressers and taxis expect a tip of about 10%. You do not have to tip if service has been poor. Bar staff (but not in pubs) may also expect a tip.

Accommodation

London has many options, ranging from the **deluxe** to homely **bed and breakfasts** (B&Bs), **hostels** and **budget hotels**. Even in the peak summer season there is rarely a shortage of places to stay but the problem is one of cost: London is an expensive city, and this is more than reflected in the price of hotel rooms.

Accommodation agencies:

PUBLIC HOLIDAYS

1 January •
New Year's Day
Late March/early April •
Good Friday and
Easter Monday
First Monday in May •
May Day Holiday
Last Monday in May •
Spring Bank Holiday
Last Monday in August •
Summer Bank Holiday
25 December •
Christmas Day
26 December •
Boxing Day

The **London Tourist Board** has some 500 hotels and guest houses on their books within a 20km radius of the capital. There is a booking fee of £5 and a deposit (deducted from your hotel bill). Reservations can be made at all three LTB centres (see p. 122) or by credit card, tel: (0171) 932-2020.

British Hotels Reservation Centres (BHRC) have branches at Heathrow and Stansted airports, and Victoria coach and train stations. Bookings are free.

Thomas Cook has hotel reservation desks at Gatwick, King's Cross, Paddington and Victoria stations; bookings carry a £4 fee.

Hotels and B&Bs: Hotels are classified according to a 'crown' system (similar to star), with ratings depending on facilities. These determine categories but give no indication of character or style. Establishments with 4 or more rooms are required to display notices of charges, and whether this includes breakfast, service charges, VAT and so on. In the off-peak winter season,

negotiate a discount if you're staying for several days, but bargaining is not the norm. Many upmarket hotels offer special weekend rates to fill rooms usually occupied by weekday business guests, so look into these mini-packages if you want to treat yourself to a weekend in a smart hotel. Most of the top hotels are centred around Knightsbridge, Mayfair and Belgravia. A room in the famous Dorchester or Claridges will cost £250–300 per night, with a level of service commensurate with the price. International chains, catering for business clients, such as the Hilton, Inter-Continental and Marriott are in a similar bracket.

Bed and Breakfasts are a relative bargain in price terms; charges in central areas are about £50 for a double room including a traditional English breakfast – if you don't mind travelling into the city every day you can find them cheaper (£20) in outlying suburbs.

Self-catering apartments offer good value for families at about £150 per week; the London Tourist Board can advise on what's available.

Eating Out

London restaurants cater to every taste and budget – the diversity is almost unmatched by any other capital city. Even traditional **British** cooking, once a by-word for stodgy food, has been revitalized by a new generation of chefs and can now hold its own against the classic cuisines. **French**, **Italian** and **Greek** restaurants are all fairly common, and have recently been joined by the spread of **Spanish** tapas and innumerable **Thai** restaurants. Britain has long been known for its ethnic foods, particularly **Chinese** and **Indian**, and **Malaysian**, **Turkish** and **Lebanese** restaurants are all found here. In recent years **pub** food has improved enormously, and while it may be hard to find a freshly-made sandwich in some areas, in others the range and quality of bar food is as good as some restaurants. There are also a number of **bistros** and **wine bars**, where as well as sampling a range of fine wines you can find light meals, salads, and other fare. If all else fails, a simple **café** or **tea-room** can provide snacks, sandwiches or a quick meal.

Transport

London Underground and London Buses operate a 24hr telephone service for travel information, tel: (0171) 222-1234. **Travel Information Centres** can provide useful free leaflets and pocket maps on bus and tube services; they are located at Oxford Circus, Piccadilly Circus, Hammersmith and St James's Park tube stations and at Euston, Victoria, King's Cross and Liverpool Street mainline stations, as well as in all four terminals at Heathrow Airport. If you're planning on using public transport extensively during the course of a day it's worth investing in a **Travelcard**, valid during off-peak times only (from 09:30 weekdays, all day at weekends)

but good value compared to individual tickets (costs of travelcard are from £3.50 for two central zones; this compares to single-journey tickets of £1.10 in zone 1, £1.40 for zones 1 & 2, and £3.20 for all zones). Even better value is a **weekly travelcard**, for which you will need a **photo-card** (these are available free on production of a passport photo at any ticket office). Costs start at £13 for one central zone. Overseas visitors can also apply for a **Visitor Travelcard**, which covers all zones for a 3, 4 or 7 day period: these are only available through overseas offices of the British Tourist Authority.

Business Hours

Most **shops** are open 09:30–17:30 Mon–Sat, although different areas have their own late-night shopping days (Wednesdays in Knightsbridge, Thursday in Oxford Street, etc). Large supermarket chains tend to stay open until 20:00 Mon–Sat, and small corner shops (similar to convenience stores) stay open until 22:00 or later. Sunday trading is now

firmly established in London, with supermarkets and some of the department stores open until 16:00.

Office hours are usually 09:30–17:30, Mon–Fri (for **banks** see under **Money Matters** on p. 122). Office workers usually have a lunch break between 13:00–14:00. **Museums** and other **tourist attractions** are usually open 09:30–18:00, Mon–Sat (closing earlier in winter), and Sundays and public holidays (10:00– 14:00 or 16:00). Many privately run attractions are open later than the state museums.

On **public holidays** (sometimes known locally as Bank Holidays) many shops and restaurants may remain open, with the exception of **Christmas Day** when almost everything is closed.

Time

During the winter Britain is on **Greenwich Mean Time** (GMT), and during the summer (from March to October) on **British Summer Time** (BST) which is one hour forward of GMT.

CONVERSION CHART		
From	**To**	**Multiply By**
Millimetres	Inches	0.0394
Metres	Yards	1.0936
Metres	Feet	3.281
Kilometres	Miles	0.6214
Kilometres square	Square miles	0.386
Hectares	Acres	2.471
Litres	Pints	1.760
Kilograms	Pounds	2.205
Tonnes	Tons	0.984
To convert Celsius to Fahrenheit: x 9 ÷ 5 + 32		

Europe:
GMT plus 1hr.
USA, Canada (East):
GMT minus 5hrs.
USA, Canada (West):
GMT minus 8hrs.
Australia:
GMT plus 8–10hrs.
New Zealand:
GMT plus 12hrs.
South Africa:
GMT plus 2hrs.

Communications

Post: Post offices are
generally open 09:00–17:30,
Mon–Fri; 09:00–12:30 or
13:00, Sat. The Trafalgar
Square Post Office (24–28
William IV Street) is open
08:00–20:00, Mon–Thurs and
Sat; 08:30-20:00, Fri. **Postage
stamps** can be bought at post
office counters, from vending
machines, and in many
newsagents.
Telephones: Public **payphones** are operated by
British Telecom (BT) and
are either coin-operated or,
increasingly, card-operated:
phonecards are available
from post offices and
newsagents and come in
denominations of £3, £5, £10
and £20.Some payphones also
accept credit cards.
London has two area codes:
0171 for numbers in Inner
London, 0181 for those in
Outer London. You will not
need the prefix if you are
dialling from within the
same area (if you are unsure,
you can use it anyway and
still be connected). Try not to
use the telephone in your
hotel room: mark-ups are
among the world's highest.

To make an international call,
dial 00, the country code
and then the area code:
Australia 61
USA & Canada 1
Ireland 353
New Zealand 64
France 33
Singapore 65
Hong Kong 852
South Africa 27

Operator assistance 100
International Operator 155
Directory assistance 192
**International directory
assistance** 153

GOOD READING

• Duncan, Andrew
(1995) *Secret London.*
New Holland, London.
Explores little-known and
hidden facets of the capital,
with 20 miles of walks.
• Duncan, Andrew
(1991) *Walking London.*
New Holland, London.
Features 30 original walks
in and around the capital.
• Porter, Roy. *London:
A Social History.* Hamish
Hamilton. Engaging and
comprehensive account of
the capital's development.
• Tames, Richard (1992)
*Traveller's History of
London.* Windrush Press.
A lively and compact
account of the capital's
history, from Londinium
to Docklands.
• Hamilton, Patrick.
*20,000 Streets Under
the Sky.* Hogarth/Trafalgar.
Romantic trilogy set in the
sleazy Soho of the 1930s.

Electricity

The current is 240 volts AC
(50 Hz). Most American or
European appliances will
need an adaptor (ask your
hotel if they can lend you one,
otherwise try a pharmacist or
an electrical shop).

Weights and Measures

The imperial system of
measurements has officially
been replaced by the metric
system, but change is slow
and most people still use the
old system. You will usually
find that shops display goods
in both metric and imperial.

Health Precautions

No special health precautions
are necessary. Most European
countries (and some in the
Commonwealth) have recip-
rocal health arrangements
should you need treatment
at an NHS hospital; you will
need to obtain the relevant
forms before you leave home.
For other nationalities,
accident and emergency
care is generally free at NHS
hospitals' casualty departments,
but other medical treatment
(including hospitalization) will
be charged for. It's therefore
advisable to arrange comprehensive travel insurance
before you leave home.

Personal Safety

Compared to many capital
cities, London is a relatively safe
destination and the greatest
risk is from thieves and pick-
pockets hanging around busy
shopping streets or on crowded underground platforms or
trains. Use common sense.

• Don't carry more cash than you will need for the day.

• Keep your wallet or purse out of sight; keep handbags fastened and don't carry a wallet in your back pocket.

• Never leave a handbag, suitcase, or coat unattended.

• Avoid poorly lit areas (such as parks) after dark.

If you are subject to a mugging or robbery, report it to the local police station (see under 'Police' in the phone book or call Directory Enquiries on 192).

Emergencies

The familiar image of the British 'bobby' plodding the streets endures, although they are an increasingly rare sight as patrol cars now dominate. Nevertheless, the police are generally approachable and helpful should you be lost or in trouble. In an emergency for police, fire or ambulance dial 999

Disabled Access

Contact: Access Project, 39 Bradley Gardens, W13 8HE or Unit for Disabled Passengers, 17 Buckingham Palace Road, SW1N 9TN, tel: (0171) 918 3312

Etiquette

London tends to be an easy-going place with very few formal dress codes or similar restrictions. A night at the opera or in a really top-class restaurant will, of course, necessitate more formal wear, but otherwise smart, casual clothes will do almost everywhere. The British are inveterate believers in **queueing**,

---

FESTIVALS

1 January • London Parade
Late Jan/early Feb • Chinese New Year
March • Chelsea Antiques Fair
Easter • Easter Parade
Kite Festival
Late March/early April •
Oxford and Cambridge Boat Race
April • London Marathon
May • Chelsea Flower Show
June • Beating the Retreat
Kenwood Concerts
Royal Academy Summer Exhibition
Derby Day
Trooping the Colour
July • Royal Tournament
City of London Festival
August • Great British Beer Festival
Notting Hill Carnival
September • Festival of Street Theatre
Horseman's Sunday
October • Costermongers Harvest Festival
Horse of the Year Show
November • Lord Mayor's Show
Guy Fawkes Night
State Opening of Parliament
Festival of Remembrance
London Film Festival
December • Christmas Lights
New Year's Eve

• For a full rundown on what's happening get hold of the London Events booklet from the London Tourist Board; for what's happening in any particular week, check the listings magazine Time Out or the Evening Standard.

---

whether it be at a bus stop, in shops or elsewhere, and don't take kindly to those not prepared to stand in line for their turn. The exception is during the rush hour on tubes, buses and trains, when a free-for-all is more likely to prevail. On the Underground you stand on the right on escalators, and keep the left clear. In recent years **smoking** has become less acceptable in public places and is now totally banned on all **public transport** and in most public buildings. Restaurants and some hotels are now also increasingly anti-smoking: check first before booking.